AF244287

DUMB LUCK

DUMB LUCK

Fuat Kircaali

First published by SYS-CON Books 2026

Copyright © 2026 by Fuat Kircaali
All rights reserved.

No part of this publication may be reproduced, stored, or transmitted in any form or by any means, electronic, mechanical, photocopying, recording, scanning, or otherwise without written permission from the publisher. It is illegal to copy this book, post it to a website, or distribute it by any other means without permission.

First edition

ISBN: 978-1-886141-02-5

Published by SYS-CON Books
New Jersey, USA
www.sys-con.com

Cover design by Louis Cuffari

I dedicate this book to my parents, whose memories guide me, and to my precious daughter, Sofia.

Contents

Author's Note

This book is based on the author's personal recollections and experiences. Some events, timelines, and dialogue have been reconstructed for narrative clarity and may not reflect exact word-for-word accounts.

Certain names and identifying details have been changed to protect privacy. Any resemblance to persons not explicitly identified is coincidental.

The views expressed are solely those of the author and do not represent the views of any organization referenced. This book is not intended as legal, financial, marital, or business advice — seriously, don't try this at home.

Any errors or omissions are unintentional and remain the author's responsibility.

"It's an incredible story. At times I got goosebumps — I was genuinely excited to keep reading.

This book has all the ingredients of a great Hollywood screenplay."

— Cem Özbatur

"I am halfway through DUMB LUCK. It is a page turner. Well done!"

Nezih Erdogan
Professor of Film Studies

PROLOGUE

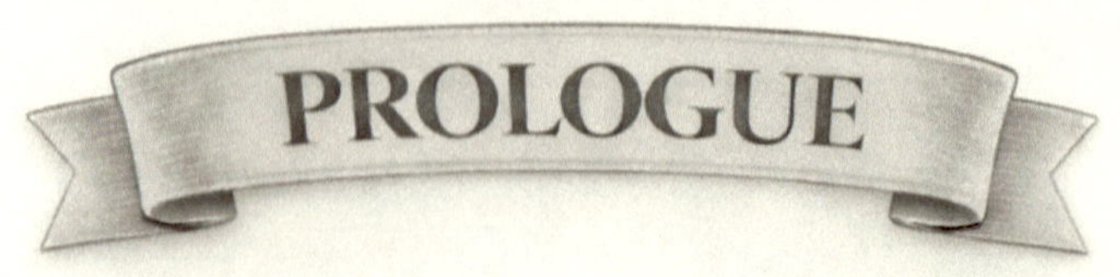

Twenty years

Two hundred million dollars

One question

How did it all happen?

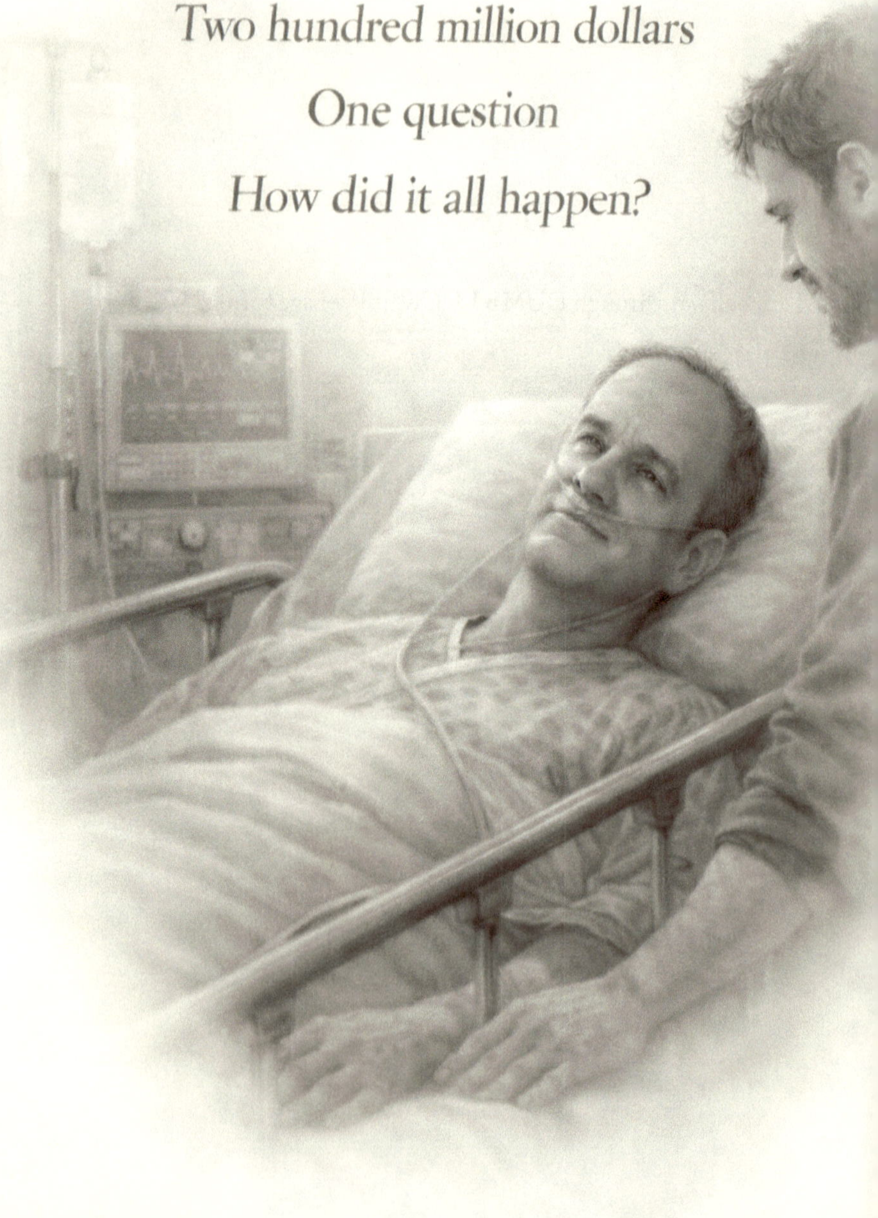

Prologue

The Number

"Mr. Kircaali," the woman said, studying her screen, "we've begun processing your Social Security retirement benefits, but there appears to be a problem."

That alone should have worried me.

She turned the monitor slightly, as if she wanted me to see the mistake for myself.

"When we add everything up," she continued, "your reported lifetime earnings come to approximately two hundred million dollars."

I looked at the number.

Did the math quickly in my head.

"Well," I said, "that's about ten million a year. Sounds right."

She froze.

Not politely.

Not professionally.

She just stopped moving.

Her eyes lifted slowly from the screen to my face, as if she were trying to reconcile two things that clearly did not belong together — the number in front of her and the man sitting across the desk.

I didn't help matters.

I never do.

I was wearing old sneakers, wrinkled jeans, and a jacket that had seen better decades. I've always had the unfortunate ability to look unemployed, regardless of circumstances.

She cleared her throat.

"Sir," she said carefully, "most people don't... say that."

I smiled.

That wasn't the first time someone had asked me that question.

* * *

Several years earlier, we were in California for CloudEXPO.

I had just arrived at the Santa Clara Convention Center when one of my staff rushed toward me.

"Fuat — Roger was taken by ambulance. Stanford Hospital."

Roger Strukhoff was our conference chair. Brilliant. Tireless. The kind of man who made everything run without needing credit for it.

I drove straight to the hospital.

* * *

He was lying in the emergency room, wires everywhere, monitors chirping softly. As nurses prepared to wheel him away for tests, he lifted his hand.

"Wait," he said.

They stopped.

He turned his head toward me and smiled — weakly, but unmistakably his.

"If I don't make it," he said, "I have one last question for you."

I leaned in.

"How the hell did you manage to eat two hundred million dollars in twenty years?"

It wasn't accusation.

It was curiosity — the kind that shows up when someone thinks they might be out of time.

I didn't have an answer then.

I still don't have one now.

I never set out to build a $200 million company.

I didn't have a strategy deck.

I didn't have a five-year plan.

I didn't raise venture capital or chase valuations.

* * *

I didn't even know what kind of company I was building until years after it already existed.

What I had was motion.

I kept saying yes before I fully understood the question.

Yes to printing magazines before I had money.

Yes to selling ads before I knew what a media kit was.

Yes to conferences before I knew how you actually ran one.

Most of the time, I wasn't planning.

I was reacting.

Momentum arrived not because I deserved it — but because I didn't stop long enough to talk myself out of things.

This book is not about brilliance.

It's not about genius.

And it's definitely not about doing everything right.

It's about what happens when you keep moving forward long enough that life runs out of chances to stop you.

* * *

People like to call that luck.

They say, "You were in the right place at the right time."

Maybe.

But timing doesn't move itself.

Luck doesn't answer the phone at two in the morning.

Luck doesn't sleep on office floors.

Luck doesn't show up when fear would have been reasonable.

I didn't get lucky.

I just didn't quit.

And somehow, over twenty years of accidents, coincidences, bad decisions, good instincts, and relentless forward motion, the number kept growing.

Until one day, a government office printed it neatly on a piece of paper and slid it across a desk.

Two hundred million dollars.

That's when I realized I probably owed an explanation.

So let me take you back to the beginning.

ACT I — THE IMMIGRANT WITH NO PLAN

I arrived with no roadmap.

No money. No network. No certainty that I even belonged here.

What I did have was motion — the instinct to keep moving forward before fear could catch up. I followed instructions, took buses, made phone calls, slept where I could, and said yes to things I didn't yet understand.

This act is not about ambition.

It's about survival.

Before there was a company, before there was money, before anyone knew my name, there was only one question that mattered:

How long could I keep going without stopping?

CHAPTER 1

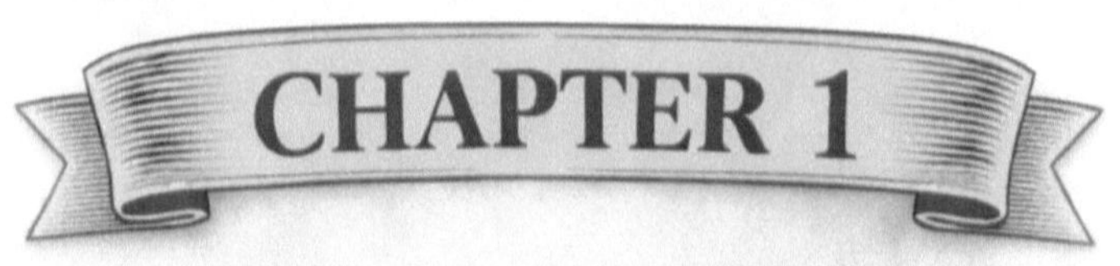

One flight from Zurich
No money
No plan.
Just a one-way
ticket to America.

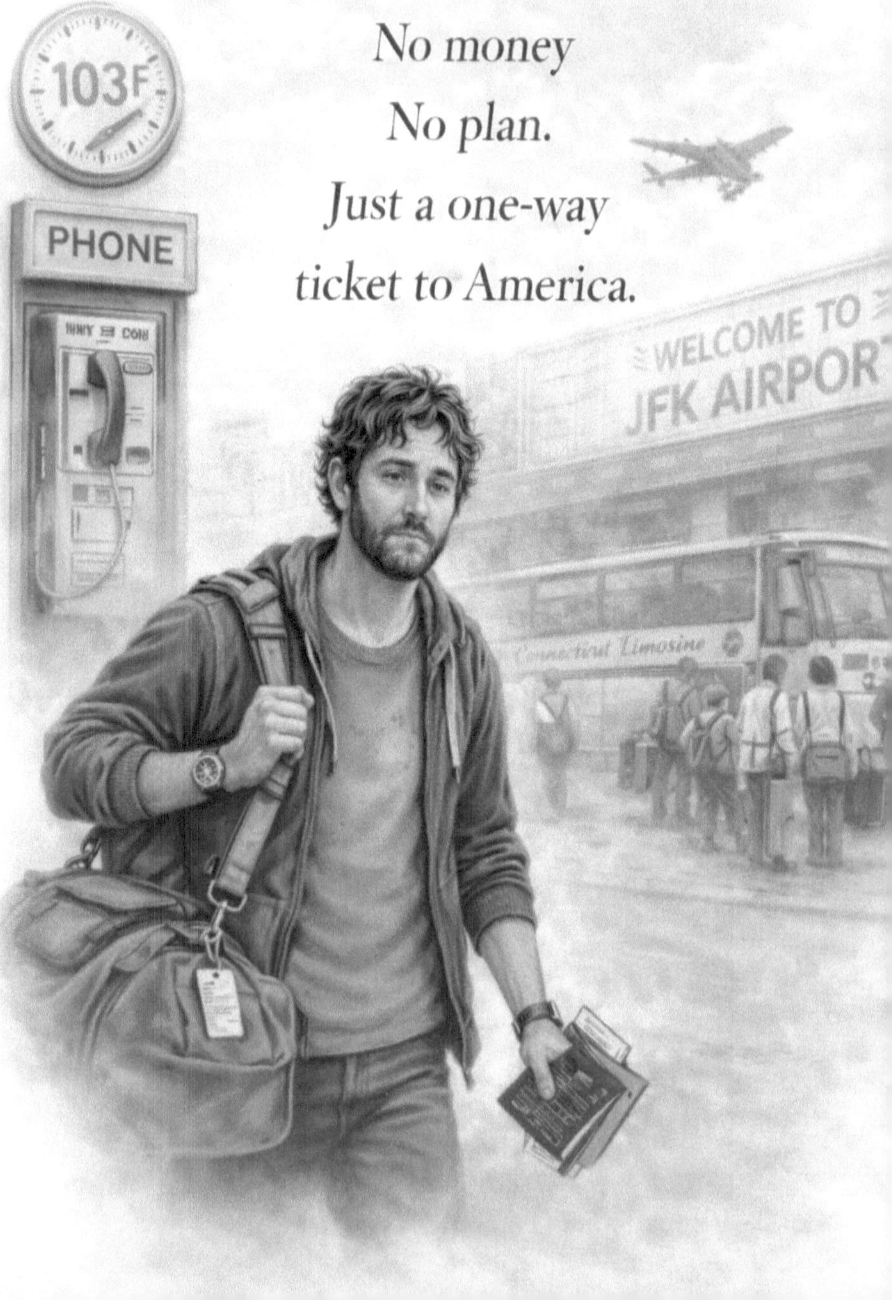

June 13, 1984 —JFK

I arrived in the United States on June 13, 1984.

I landed at JFK Airport from Zurich, Switzerland, on what turned out to be the hottest day of the century. The *Hartford Courant* later ran a headline announcing the temperature — 103 degrees.

I didn't need the paper to tell me that.

The heat announced itself the moment I stepped outside.

* * *

I followed instructions.

I waited for the Connecticut Limousine bus, boarded it, and rode to Hartford. When the bus stopped at Valley's Steak House, I got off, walked to a payphone, dropped in a quarter, and dialed the number I had been given.

Mary Wrobleski answered.

She arrived with her mother, Mrs. Wrobleski, and drove me to the house where I would live for the next eighteen months.

I didn't ask many questions.

At that stage, forward motion was enough.

My two roommates were Gilberto Acosta from Brazil and Judith Olgado from the Isle of Man. Judith's mother was Filipino. Her father was British.

The household felt like an international experiment — one that worked mostly because no one was particularly attached to being comfortable.

Two years earlier, I had been accepted into the PhD program in Computer Science at the University of Zurich. The university did not award separate master's degrees. The Licentiate — Lic. oec. — was considered equivalent.

When I met with admissions, they asked about my background. I told them I had just graduated from Boğaziçi University in Istanbul with a Bachelor of Arts in Business Administration.

"That's a very good school," one of them said.

"One of the top two hundred universities in the world."

That mattered to me then.

Credentials always do — until they don't.

* * *

During my studies, I chose a computer programming course taught in Pascal. The professor was Niklaus Wirth — the man who had created the language himself.

Pascal wasn't just code.

It was discipline.
Structure.
Precision.

If you were sloppy, the system punished you immediately.
If you were clear, it rewarded you just as fast.

Wirth had designed Pascal around 1970 at ETH Zurich, naming it after the mathematician Blaise Pascal. He later created Modula-2 and Oberon, and received the Turing Award in 1984 — the same year I landed in America.

At the time, I had no idea how long his influence would stay with me.

* * *

Two years into my doctoral program, I received an unexpected job offer through AIESEC.

The description was short — almost vague.

The project was in Bloomfield, Connecticut, and was expected to last about eighteen months.

The job involved designing a spare-parts inventory system for SH-2 Seasprite submarine-hunter helicopters at Kaman Aerospace Corporation, a major U.S. Navy contractor.

I didn't fully understand what the work would involve.

After class one day, I showed the offer to Professor Wirth. He read it carefully and said the company likely already had established hardware and software systems.

"You'll probably just be drawing flowcharts for the programming team," he said.
"Nothing too involved."

That turned out to be optimistic.

* * *

Kaman Aerospace was headquartered in Bloomfield and had been founded in 1945 by Charles H. Kaman, an aviation pioneer known for his unconventional helicopter designs.

The SH-2 Seasprite had evolved from a small utility aircraft into a full anti-submarine warfare platform used by the U.S. Navy's LAMPS program.

During my time there, the IT director was Bill Harrop. Reporting to him was Vaughan Marecki, a senior figure in the department.

* * *

After delivering the inventory system successfully, I accepted a position with IBM in their Information Systems and Communications Group at 44 South Broadway in White Plains, New York.

My role was to produce weekly market research reports on printers and peripherals for senior management.

That office reported up through Michael Armstrong — who would later become CEO of AT&T.

IBM was enormous.

Impressive.

And already quietly shedding people.

Around 1985, IBM introduced an early retirement program designed to reduce headcount. Full-time positions became harder to secure.

Eventually, mine disappeared.

Without a job, I moved from White Plains to Hoboken, New Jersey.

A childhood friend — someone I had gone to high school and college with — was working toward his PhD in physics at Stevens Institute of Technology.

He had a dorm room.

At night, he snuck me in after hours. I slept in empty beds and disappeared during the day.

We were broke.

We bought a gallon of milk for ninety-nine cents and a bag of flour and made yogurt and bread to last the week.

* * *

On Saturday nights, *The New York Times* delivered the full Sunday edition to newsstands.

I paid one dollar for the Help Wanted section and took it home.

I started alphabetically.

Computers.
Software.

By Sunday morning, my cover letters and résumés were already in the mail.

Some Sundays, I hand-delivered them instead. Offices were quiet.

No one stopped you.

* * *

After months of searching, I was offered a PC analyst position at Movado Watch Company.

The salary — $20,000 a year — barely covered the bus fare from Hoboken to the Port Authority.

But it was a job.

And Movado promised to sponsor my green card.

That promise, like many others I would hear later, turned out to be empty.

But at the time, I didn't know that.

I was just relieved to be moving forward again.

CHAPTER 2

Four years before Marc Benioff

I built the sales automation system

No investors

No one knew

My Last Real Job

I lost my job in the early 1990s when UWCC, a clinical weight-loss company, went out of business. United Weight Loss had been founded by Ed Saltzman, a serial entrepreneur who put together a strong management team that included Steven Silk as CEO. I reported directly to Steve as the company's MIS director.

Steve would later become the CEO of Hebrew National, where he helped guide the brand from its roots as a New York kosher butcher into a nationally recognized premium hot dog company—selling quality, tradition, and the famous promise that it "answered to a higher authority."

At UWCC, Steve's big dream was to get the company listed on the *Inc. 500* as one of America's fastest-growing private companies.

That never happened.

A few years later, though, life showed its sense of humor. My own company, SYS-CON Media, would make the *Inc. 500* list three years in a row.

The timing couldn't have been worse. The recession hit, UWCC never became profitable, and Ed eventually pulled the plug. Steve and the rest of the management team left—and I left with them.

Suddenly I had no job and no plan.

***

What followed was nearly a year of rejection.

I applied to just about every computer and software development job in the tri-state area and landed only a handful of interviews. On paper, the 1990–1991 recession didn't last long, but in real life it dragged on.

Banks were failing after the Savings and Loan disaster.

Credit was tight.

Oil prices spiked after Iraq invaded Kuwait.

Even when the recession was officially declared "over," jobs were still scarce.

It felt like the economy had moved on without telling anyone still looking for work.

After almost nine months of searching, I finally landed a job as a PC systems developer at the French chemical company Rhône-Poulenc in Cranbury, New Jersey.

I was their first—and only—"PC guy," and it showed.

When I arrived, they actually had to scramble to find me a computer. Until then everything ran on mainframes and minicomputers. PCs weren't part of the plan, and no one was quite sure how—or if—they were supposed to fit in.

The job was a break.

But it came with a new problem: the commute.

I was living at 46 Holly Street in Jersey City and driving all the way down to Cranbury every day. With rush-hour traffic, it took about ninety minutes each way, which I could live with.

What I couldn't live with was the toll.

The New Jersey Turnpike cost $2.85 each way, plus gas—about $300 a month I simply didn't have.

Eventually I found a workaround: entering the Turnpike in Elizabeth, which dropped the toll to just thirty-five cents each way.

Over less than three years at Rhône-Poulenc, I put more than 70,000 miles on my Honda Civic.

Proof that sometimes survival isn't about speed or comfort.

It's just about finding a way to keep moving forward.

***

In the early 1990s, when I started working at Rhône-Poulenc, RPG—Report Program Generator—was everywhere.

Their IT department didn't know anything else.

It quietly ran the day-to-day business: payroll, inventory, manufacturing, accounting. No one made a fuss about it.

Most of the RPG code was written in rigid fixed-format columns, tightly bound to the operating system and database. The code wasn't pretty, but the systems were incredibly fast and reliable.

Those RPG applications just worked—year after year.

Many of the programs they depended on were already old back then, and they still felt indestructible.

Around this time, I developed and rolled out what was effectively the company's first sales-force automation system—almost a decade before Marc Benioff would make the idea famous.

I'm no genius.

As a PC systems developer, my favorite tool—the one I really got good at—was Paradox from Borland.

I was so into it that I subscribed to several monthly journals published by a company called the COBB Group, including *Paradox User's Journal* and *Paradox Developer's Journal*.

These weren't glossy magazines.

They were printed in black-and-white, scientific-journal style—the kind that looked serious enough to scare non-programmers.

The subscription wasn't cheap either: $119 a year for twelve issues.

A few years later, when I launched my first magazine, *PowerBuilder Developer's Journal*, I shamelessly copied that exact format and even reused the same $119 price point.

Why mess with a model that already worked?

***

At the time, Borland Paradox was one of the most popular desktop relational databases around, especially in the late 1980s and early 1990s.

My colleagues at Rhône-Poulenc had never heard of PC tools like this. It was a completely foreign world to them.

Paradox made serious database work feel almost friendly.

It bundled a real relational database with forms, reports, and a built-in programming language all in one place. Non-programmers could design tables and run queries, while developers could use ObjectPAL to build surprisingly sophisticated business applications in record time.

On DOS—and later Windows—Paradox earned a reputation for being fast, stable, and extremely developer-friendly.

It was ideal for departmental systems, internal tools, prototypes, and standalone business applications—the kind that quietly ran companies while nobody paid much attention to them.

In the early 1990s, Paradox went head-to-head with dBASE and Microsoft Access. Technically it was strong, but momentum matters.

Once Microsoft bundled Access with Office and the industry shifted toward client-server databases like Oracle and SQL Server, Paradox slowly faded from the spotlight.

Still, it left a lasting mark.

It proved how powerful desktop databases could be and trained an entire generation of developers—including me—to think in relational terms long before web apps and cloud databases were even imaginable.

***

After Paradox, the next tool that completely grabbed me was PowerBuilder.

In the early 1990s, right around the time I started at Rhône-Poulenc, it felt like the future had finally arrived.

Built by Powersoft and later acquired by Sybase, PowerBuilder made it possible to build serious, corporate-grade Windows applications without drowning in C or low-level code.

I knew I had to get my hands on PowerBuilder.

But it wasn't cheap.

A typical developer license cost between $3,000 and $5,000 per seat.

I convinced my boss, Randy Hompesch, to buy a copy—and he did.

The problem was that PowerBuilder was so new and so revolutionary that there were no courses, books, or formal training programs.

You learned it by doing.

What made PowerBuilder feel almost magical was the DataWindow.

You could visually design a screen, connect it to a database, and suddenly you had querying, updating, validation, and reporting all working together.

Things that used to take weeks—or sometimes months—could be built in days.

For enterprise developers, it was a revelation.

PowerBuilder had been created by David Litwack, who founded Powersoft and designed the original architecture. His breakthrough idea—the DataWindow—dramatically simplified building database-driven applications and set PowerBuilder apart from everything else at the time.

By the time Sybase acquired Powersoft, PowerBuilder was already the dominant client-server development tool of the 1990s.

It quickly became the go-to platform inside large corporate IT departments, especially in finance, insurance, telecom, healthcare, and manufacturing.

If you walked into a serious IT shop in the mid-1990s, odds were good that PowerBuilder was running something mission-critical.

***

DUMB LUCK ENVIRONMENT IN MY KITCHEN

While all of this was happening at work, life at home was unraveling.

I took a leave of absence, went to Turkey, completed my three months of basic military service in the mountains, and then returned to New Jersey.

When I came home, the apartment was empty.

Everything was gone.

Clothes from the closets.

Shirts and underwear from the bedroom drawers.

Furniture.

Window treatments.

Everything.

I called the Jersey City police and reported a burglary.

I explained that I had been overseas for three months, had just returned, and found the apartment completely stripped.

Two officers walked through the place in silence.

After a few minutes, one of them looked at me and said:

"Nothing's been stolen. It looks like your wife left you."

***

I really didn't want to live alone.

So I invited a friend who was working toward his PhD in physics at Stevens Institute of Technology in Hoboken and offered him one of the two bedrooms.

He moved in.

During our late-night conversations at the apartment, I told him about this new client-server platform called PowerBuilder.

"There's a huge buzz around it," I said. "It looks like it's going to take over."

I needed to learn PowerBuilder, get a better job, and finally end my miserable commute.

The problem was that there were no educational tools.

No courses.

No books.

No clear way to master it.

This wasn't something you could just install on a PC and study in isolation like Paradox. You needed a real back-end server to connect to.

And that was the irony.

The one place where I could actually do this—at work—was an environment still coding everything in RPG.

For God's sake.

***

This was all before the internet, at least as we know it today.

There was AOL, though.

You could connect with a 1200-baud modem—something you could buy at 47th Street Photo in Manhattan—and wait patiently as it screamed its way online.

While poking around, I discovered the Powersoft bulletin board.

It was an official dial-up BBS run by Powersoft in the early 1990s, long before web forums existed.

PowerBuilder developers connected by modem to download patches and sample code, read technical notes, and exchange messages with other users—and occasionally with Powersoft engineers themselves.

It was part technical support, part knowledge base, and part community.

For many developers it was the only practical way to learn PowerBuilder beyond pure trial and error.

Long before Stack Overflow, blogs, or online documentation, that bulletin board was where serious PowerBuilder developers went to survive—and level up.

***

This was the most exciting thing that had happened to me since my wife's disappearance a couple of months earlier.

I spent several nights standing for hours at my kitchen counter.

The modem cable to the only phone jack in the house wasn't long enough to put my Macintosh Classic on the table, so I had to stand there while connecting.

I was trying to find a *PowerBuilder Developer's Journal*—something like my two favorite magazines, *Paradox User's Journal* and *Paradox Developer's Journal*.

I had subscribed to them for years.

I saved every single issue.

They were the most valuable things on my bookshelf—mostly because I didn't actually own a bookshelf, but you get the idea.

I posted exactly two questions on the Powersoft bulletin board.

First:

"Are there any PowerBuilder magazines out there?"

A couple of people replied.

No.

Then I asked:

"Is there a PowerBuilder book I can buy?"

Again, a few responses came back.

No.

That was… disappointing.

***

Late one night my friend came downstairs to the kitchen to pour himself some coffee.

"Any luck finding a way to learn PowerBuilder?" he asked.

"No," I said. "There's nothing out there. Zip. Zilch. I miss my Paradox journals."

Then a lightbulb went on.

"Wait," I said. "Why don't we start a magazine and publish a book ourselves? People need this. This is the hottest thing in IT since COBOL."

He stared at me.

"What do you know about PowerBuilder?"

"Absolutely nothing," I said.

He didn't hesitate.

"Don't get my name involved. You're on your own. I've got a few months left to finish my PhD and I don't want any part of this."

I tried one last time.

"We'll be fifty-fifty partners. Just hear me out."

That didn't help.

If anything, the idea itself seemed to stress him out.

I finally gave up trying to convince my childhood friend and roommate.

That night, right before bed, I posted my third message on the bulletin board:

"Announcing *PowerBuilder Developer's Journal*. Respond to this message to receive your sample copy."

At that point, I figured the worst thing that could happen was more silence.

***

The next morning I woke up early and drove my battle-scarred 1985 Honda Civic to work.

I convinced my boss, Randy, to let me generate daily sales reports using Paradox on a PC.

He looked at me and said:

"You're useless with the RPG tasks I give you anyway. Go ahead—make my day."

That was all the permission I needed.

Paradox was my weapon of choice.

Before lunch I dropped three different flavors of sales reports—by sales manager—on his desk.

His eyes went wide.

"How did you do that?" he asked. "And what is this Paradox thing you're using?"

I told him Paradox was king.

Fast. Relational. No need to fart around with RPG just to answer a simple question.

I came from the relational world—tables, structure, normalization.

Mainframe guys didn't even know what that meant yet.

To them, data was something you wrestled with.

To me, it was something you disciplined.

In the relational universe, normalization isn't optional.

It's law.

One fact. One place.

Break that rule and the data lies to you.

Follow it, and it tells the truth—even when the system gets big, ugly, and expensive.

***

Here's what actually happened during my short stint at Rhône-Poulenc.

I singled out Larry, the top salesman in the Animal Nutrition division down in Atlanta.

Larry was different.

While most people in the early '90s were still allergic to PCs, Larry was inseparable from his Compaq LTE. He carried it like it was part of his body.

Larry was also one of the few salespeople who truly needed data to do his job.

He kept pushing the MIS department for timely sales reports—numbers he could actually use while the week was still alive.

What he got instead was a ritual straight out of the Stone Age.

Once a week, someone printed the reports, stuffed them in an envelope, and mailed them to him.

By the time those reports landed on Larry's desk, they were already history.

And everyone acted like this was normal.

I sat down with him and asked for his top ten reports—the ones he actually cared about.

I told him I'd deliver the information overnight, online, straight to his Compaq.

And if he wanted paper, he could print it at home.

He looked at me and asked:

"How?"

I said, "Give me a few weeks. You'll have a sales-force automation system running on your PC."

He was excited—but skeptical.

Honestly, I couldn't blame him.

***

In the early '90s, 9,600 baud was considered fast—almost luxurious.

If you were coming from 2,400 baud, jumping to 9,600 felt like the future had arrived.

Screens updated smoothly.

Email didn't crawl line by line.

You could almost convince yourself the system was real-time.

I installed a rack of ten modems in my office.

On paper, that was more than enough for a hundred salesmen to dial in and pull their reports.

We built and rolled out my Paradox-based sales-force automation system straight to Larry's Compaq.

And while I was at it, I gave him email too.

Eudora.

Larry, being Larry, couldn't keep it to himself.

He started showing off his live sales data to other salesmen and casually bragging about his email like it was a new sports car.

Word spread fast.

Before long, Randy—my boss—showed up in my office and asked what I had done for the salesman in Atlanta.

I said:

"Larry gets all his sales reports online. He dials in, updates his numbers daily, and has everything he needs to actually run his business."

Randy had heard of email.

But in his mind email meant AOL.

I gave him his own company email address anyway.

That's when things started to get interesting.

***

He went and talked to his boss, Jim Purcell, about whatever strange operation seemed to be running out of my desk.

I gave Jim email too.

Jim didn't even have a PC on his desk at the time.

After that conversation, he ordered one.

What confused everyone in the department wasn't the technology.

It was the result.

Somehow, a salesman hundreds of miles away had an application on his computer that actually worked and gave him all the information he needed—when he needed it.

That simply wasn't how things were supposed to happen.

***

That same week, Randy came back to me and said he'd been getting phone calls.

Every salesman in Atlanta wanted whatever Larry had.

I told him, "No problem. We'll roll it out to all of them."

Then I asked, almost as an afterthought:

"Do you want me to order Compaqs for them?"

He said, "Please do."

About twenty salesmen—all men—got their computers.

Six thousand dollars each.

That was a $120,000 investment.

Which sounded outrageous until you realized the company now had a million-dollar sales system—one the competition didn't have.

It was a big deal.

And the department was getting credit for it all the way up the chain—from Bernie to Jim to Randy.

They were proud.

***

Remember that water-cooler conversation with my department director, Bernie Kranz, one Saturday morning?

The one where he told me I didn't fit in the corporate world and should go start my own business?

This was happening right in the middle of all that.

One day, not long after things took off with Randy, I looked up from my desk and saw Bernie standing there.

Just standing.

I knew something was up.

He said he'd been getting phone calls about my sales-force automation system—from other divisions in North America.

They wanted it too.

This wasn't some small operation.

Rhône-Poulenc was massive—the largest French company, owned by the French government, operating all over the world.

And suddenly whatever had quietly started at my desk was getting attention far beyond our little corner of the building.

Bernie skipped Jim and Randy and talked to me directly.

We rolled out my sales-force automation system to two other divisions in North America.

Guess who showed up at my desk next?

John Wistrich, the president of Specialty Chemicals North America.

"Hey John," I said.

"How are you doing, Fuat?" he replied.

"We're rolling out the system," I told him. "Everyone seems to love it. It's helping our sales teams tremendously."

He nodded.

"That's why I stopped by. I got a call from Paris this morning. The worldwide corporate MIS director is on his way here with his team."

"They want to see your demo."

I said, "We're ready. Whenever they arrive, we'll set up the presentation."

John smiled—proud, but a little nervous at the same time—then turned and walked away.

***

The French team arrived.

I presented the system to four executives from Paris, with John Wistrich,

Bernie Kranz, Jim Purcell, and Randy Hompesch—my four layers of bosses—all sitting in the room.

We turned down the lights and ran the demo.

When it was over, the senior executive from Paris spoke.

"We will roll out this system worldwide," he said.

"Starting in Argentina."

Just like that, my sales-force automation system was set to be used by the largest French company in the world.

Four years before Marc Benioff started Salesforce.com.

CHAPTER 3

"Mitchell hates people calling him Mitch.

Never call him Mitch.

Always say Mitchell."

The Man Who Jump-Started Everything

That night, right before bed, I posted my third message on the bulletin board:

"Announcing *PowerBuilder Developer's Journal*. Respond to this message to receive your sample copy!"

I hit send and went to sleep fully expecting what had become my new normal: absolutely nothing.

* * *

The next morning, I woke up early and drove my battle-scarred 1985 Honda Civic to work — a car held together by rust, hope, and unpaid parking tickets.

That evening, the moment I walked through the door, I dialed into the *Powersoft* BBS.

No dinner.
No small talk.
Straight to the modem.

OMG.
OMG.

There were thirty-six replies to the message I had posted the night before.

Thirty-six.

I stared at the screen like it had made a typo.

Then I started reading them slowly, carefully, as if they might disappear if I moved too fast. Every single one said the same thing:

Yes, send me a sample copy.

That's when my childhood friend — my roommate — walked in from Stevens Institute of Technology.

I jumped out of my chair and yelled:

"You won't believe this!"

He looked concerned.

Rightly so.

"There are thirty-six replies to my post from last night," I said.

"They all want sample copies of *PowerBuilder Developer's Journal*!"

He looked at my face, then at the screen, then back at me.

"You are now in very deep trouble."

I nodded.

"Maybe."

What I didn't say out loud was the real problem — and he knew it.

I didn't actually have a magazine.

Not a layout.
Not an editor.
Not a printer.

Not even a clue about what PowerBuilder does.

I had demand.

Which, as I was about to learn, is the most dangerous thing you can have without a plan.

And completely terrifying.

I kept reading the messages. That's when I noticed something new.

A few people weren't asking for sample copies.

They were asking if they could write articles.

That felt like skipping ten steps ahead on a staircase I hadn't even found yet.

I replied to everyone with the most professional sentence I could come up with:

"Please submit your article proposals by email to my AOL address, including screenshots."

The moment I hit send, I thought, *Wow. I sound like someone who runs a magazine.*

* * *

One name kept appearing in the forum threads.

He was everywhere — answering questions, correcting mistakes, debating features.

He clearly knew PowerBuilder better than anyone else in the room.

His name was Steve Benfield.

I sent him a private message.

"Would you be interested in being the editor?"

He replied:

"Me?
Chief editor of *PowerBuilder Developer's Journal*?"

"Yes."

There was a pause.

Then his answer came back:

"Sure. Of course."

Just like that, I had an editor.

Before he could change his mind, I posted a public message:

"Steve Benfield is the chief editor of *PowerBuilder Developer's Journal*.
Please submit all article proposals to him."

And that's how I hired my first editor.

No contracts.
No meetings.
No magazine.

Just confidence, a modem, and an AOL email address.

Somehow, it was starting to work.

Then I received a message that stopped me cold.

It was from a man named Mitchell Kertzman.

He wrote:

"Fuat, congratulations on *PowerBuilder Developer's Journal*.
How can we help?"

I typed back:

"Who are you?
How can you help?"

His reply came quickly.

"I'm the chairman of Powersoft.
Let me know how we can help you."

That was not what I was expecting.

The chairman of the company.

Offering me help.

I was shaking.

* * *

Up until that moment, my entire business plan came from one memory: every time I bought a software upgrade, there was a subscription card inside the box. That's how I subscribed to my favorite journals. So yes — I had ideas. But none of them involved talking to the chairman of Powersoft.

* * *

Steve Benfield immediately sent me a private message.

"Mitchell hates people calling him Mitch.
Never call him Mitch.
Always say Mitchell."

Understood.

A moment later, Mitchell posted again:

"We're in Boston.

Why don't you come to our office and we talk?"

And just like that, a magazine that didn't yet exist had been invited to headquarters.

* * *

Later that night, my roommate wandered into the kitchen for another cup of coffee. I gave him the update.

"I've recruited writers.
I hired an editor-in-chief.
And now the chairman of Powersoft wants to meet me."

He froze.

"So," I added, "are you sure you don't want to be fifty-fifty partners?"

He didn't hesitate.

"I'm one hundred percent sure I want no part of your dangerous midnight adventure."

Fair enough.
The problem was getting to Boston.

My Honda had already voted no.

"I need to rent a car," I said.
"Will you come with me?"

After some negotiation, he agreed — not as a partner, not as support.

Just as a witness.

At Powersoft headquarters, I was escorted into Mitchell Kertzman's office.

He gestured to a chair.

"Please, sit."

PowerBuilder 4.0 was shipping in a few weeks, he explained. Then he handed me an address.

"There's a company in Vermont that does our shrink-wrapping. Send them seventy-five thousand subscription cards. They'll insert them into the product boxes."

That was the meeting.

No pitch deck.
No committees.
No debate.

Just instructions.

The chairman of Powersoft had just given me access to seventy-five thousand customers.

* * *

Back in the car, reality returned. How was I supposed to print and ship seventy-five thousand subscription cards? I studied magazines at Barnes & Noble like blueprints. At home, I recreated the cards on my Macintosh Classic. For the mailing address, I used my townhouse:

46 Holly Street
Jersey City, NJ 07302

I printed the cards at a small shop in Chinatown — black and white, simple, affordable.

When they were ready, I boxed them up and mailed everything to Vermont.

· CHAPTER 4 ·

*"My credit card — already maxed out —
had $1,200 left for all expenses."*

$10,000 I Didn't Have

Between jobs, I was moonlighting as the local computer guy for small businesses. To look legit, I printed business cards, letterhead, and envelopes and gave the business a very official-sounding name: Systems Consultants.

One day at the weight-loss company, a programmer friend took one look at my business card and said,

"That name's way too long. Just call it SYS-CON."

I didn't argue. It sounded right.

When I decided to publish *PowerBuilder Developer's Journal*, I tweaked the name to *SYS-CON Publications*. Later — after I finally figured out how you actually register a company — it became *SYS-CON Publications, Inc.* And once conferences entered the picture, the name settled into what it would be from then on:

SYS-CON Media.

Back home, it was time to print the very first issue of *PowerBuilder Developer's Journal*.

I had Aldus PageMaker on my Macintosh, which at the time felt like cheating. Real desktop publishing, sitting right there on my kitchen counter.

I decided to make the magazine thirty-six pages — twelve pages thicker than *Paradox Developer's Journal*, which ran twenty-four pages in two colors. I picked cyan for the titles and accents.

No deep strategy.
It just felt right.

* * *

Then came the printer hunt.

I made a lot of calls before finding a Hasidic Jewish printer in Brooklyn who said he could do 10,000 copies for $10,000. It was the best deal I could find.

And that's when it hit me.

This wasn't just an idea anymore.
I was actually doing it.

My credit card — already maxed out — had $1,200 left for all expenses.

Where was I going to find ten thousand dollars?

I had a friend named Şima Uluç. Her father, Doğan Uluç, was the longtime New York bureau chief for *Hürriyet* and a well-known Turkish-American journalist.

One day in Manhattan, I met Şima for coffee and explained my problem — how I was supposed to pay for printing the magazine.

She didn't hesitate.

"It's easy," she said.
"You make a media kit and sell ads. That covers your printing costs."

I nodded like I understood.

I had absolutely no idea what a media kit was.

I was too embarrassed to ask.

It took me about a month to figure it out.

Eventually, I think I called Advisor Publications and asked them to send me one of theirs. When it arrived in the mail, things finally started to make sense.

They published magazines like *FoxPro Advisor*, *Database Advisor*, and other language-specific journals popular with software developers. You could find them right on newsstands.

Unlike my *Paradox Developer's Journal*, their magazines had ads.

Now I understood why.

* * *

I copied their media kit, tweaked it just enough so it wouldn't look identical, and mailed it to every Powersoft partner I could find — maybe thirty to fifty companies across the country.

I told them the premier issue of *PowerBuilder Developer's Journal* would debut at the Powersoft User Conference at the Dolphin at Disney World in Orlando.

This was their chance to reach the entire PowerBuilder community.

* * *

Meanwhile, I still had a full-time day job.

Between commuting and the office, I worked about ten hours a day — then stayed up most of the night building the magazine. I dropped mail at the Manhattan Main Post Office — open twenty-four hours, thankfully — and drove straight to work in South Jersey in my beat-up

Honda Civic.

Somewhere along the way, I started wondering when this had become a perfectly reasonable plan.

Remember Carmen?

I tracked down her cubicle at the office and walked over.

"Carmen, I need to talk to you," I said.
 "Don't get excited. Not to get married. I need help. I'm starting a business. Can we have lunch?"

She didn't miss a beat.

"If you're making fifty thousand dollars a year, I'll go to lunch with you."

I was heartbroken.

My salary was only thirty thousand.

* * *

MEDIA KIT MAILER MIRACLE

Within a week, the media kit mailer started producing what felt like miracles.

Out of the fifty large envelopes I'd dropped at the Manhattan Main Post Office, my phone began ringing two or three times a day.

These were real calls.
From real companies.
With real money.

PowerServe in Tampa, Florida jumped in immediately, booking the back cover for twelve issues at $3,000 per issue.

That same day, I sold the inside front cover spread to Greenbriar & Russell in Chicago — also $3,000 per issue, also a twelve-issue commitment.

The inside back cover went for $2,000.

I couldn't believe what was happening.

Over the following week, I sold ten more pages of ads for another $10,000.

At that point, I started telling people we were sold out.

Which created a new problem.

The magazine had to grow.

I increased the page count to forty-eight pages, with fifteen now dedicated to advertising.

Before laying out a single page, I had already booked $18,000 in revenue.

Printing would cost $10,000.

That left $8,000 to cover everything else.

For the first time, this didn't feel like a crazy idea anymore.

It felt real.

I went back to Carmen's desk.

"Look at these contracts," I said.
"I just sold eighteen thousand dollars' worth of ads — and I still have no idea what I'm doing."

I told her I had three months to lay out and print the magazine. For a professional designer, it would have taken a week.

For me, it was going to be a three-month crash course in panic.
And there was a hard deadline.

I had to walk into the Powersoft User Conference at Disney World in June with the first issue in my hands.

"I need help with ad sales," I said.
"And possibly adult supervision."

* * *

She came to my townhouse in Jersey City after work.

By then, my answering machine was packed with messages from all over the country. She listened for a few minutes, shook her head, and said:

"Fine. I'll take two days off, drive to your house, and organize this mess."

Those two days turned into a one-week leave of absence.

Every morning, she drove to my house to keep things under control — while I drove in the opposite direction to my day job.

We were both working full-time.

Just not on the same thing.

That was the moment I realized something important:

I wasn't starting a magazine anymore.

I was starting a company — whether I was ready or not.

CHAPTER 5

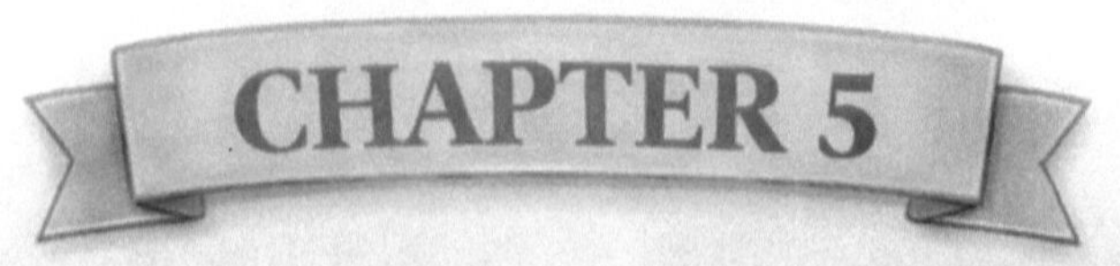

Please come to the Jersey City Post Office
to pick up mail that did not fit
in your mailbox.

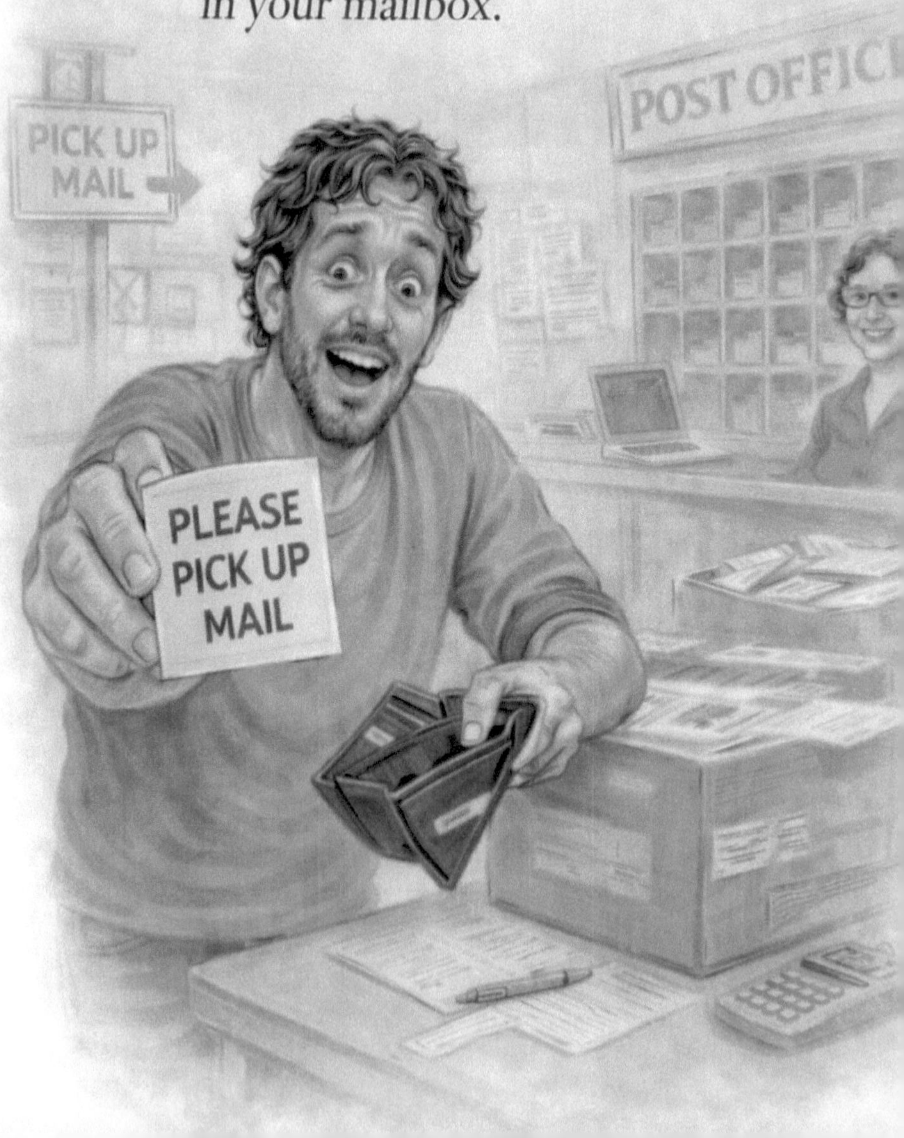

You've Got Mail

I t had been almost two months since I shipped seventy-five thousand subscription cards to a factory in Vermont, where they were being shrink-wrapped into *PowerBuilder 4.0* boxes. After that, there was nothing to do but wait.

No tracking numbers.
No confirmations.
Just faith.

* * *

One afternoon in Manhattan, I was walking past a *CompUSA* when something stopped me cold.

In the front window stood a mountain of *PowerBuilder* boxes — hundreds of them, stacked floor to ceiling like a monument. That was the official shipping day. The equivalent of an iPhone launch before anyone called it that.

I just stood there, frozen, staring at the boxes.

My cards were inside them.

All of them.

My hands started shaking.

This wasn't just another software release — it was the release. *Power-*

Builder was redefining client-server computing, and its newest version was now out in the world, rolling into offices and developer desks everywhere.

And tucked inside every shrink-wrapped box was my subscription card.

Proof that I was somehow part of this moment.

* * *

I wanted desperately to buy one — to tear it open and see it with my own eyes. But the price was nearly $3,000, money I didn't have.

So instead, I stood there on the sidewalk, staring through the glass, knowing that something extraordinary had already happened.

I didn't need to open a box to confirm it.

I was in.

* * *

That week, I moved my Macintosh upstairs into my bedroom.

I bought a small foldable table and set it up wherever it would fit — which wasn't much. Most nights, I sat on the edge of my bed, hunched over the keyboard, laying out the first issue.

It wasn't glamorous.

But it was mine.

Steve Benfield, my editor-in-chief, had selected ten authors and ten articles for the premiere issue. As soon as he accepted a piece, he sent it straight to me.

The files started trickling in one by one.

With each arrival, the magazine began to feel more real.

I settled on a three-column layout in *Aldus PageMaker*. Each article opened with a half page of breathing room, followed by text set in 11-point Times Roman and headlines in 16-point *Arial*.

The pages looked fine.

Maybe not perfect — but to my eyes, at two in the morning, sitting on the edge of my bed, they were more than acceptable.

They looked like a real magazine.

On weekends, I'd print the latest pages I'd laid out, tuck them under my arm, and take them with me to the movie theater in Newark.

I'd watch the movie, sure — but mostly I sat there flipping through the pages in the dark, admiring them like they were already published.

I couldn't help myself.

Holding them in my hands made it all feel real.

One day, in the middle of working on the first issue, I walked outside to check the mail.

Electric bill.
Gas bill.
My Chase credit card statement.
A few pieces of junk mail.

And then something different.

A small note from the post office that read:

Please come to the Jersey City Post Office to pick up mail that did not fit in your mailbox.

Curiosity got the better of me.

I jumped into my beat-up Honda Civic and drove straight to the post office. I handed the slip to the clerk.

She disappeared into the back room.

A moment later, she returned carrying a huge stack of boxes.

They were my subscription cards.

All of them.

Right there on the counter, in front of me, was proof that this wasn't just an idea anymore.

It was happening.

* * *

I ran home and dumped the pile onto the kitchen table. One by one, I started flipping through the subscription cards.

They were all filled out — names, addresses, credit card numbers, expiration dates. Everything.

This was the early 1990s. There were no fraud alerts. No identity-theft panic. People simply wrote their credit card numbers on a card, dropped it in the mail, and trusted the system.

Trusted me.

* * *

I counted them slowly, afraid I'd misread something.

Five hundred twenty-three subscription cards.

At $119 each. I did the math twice. $62,237.

There it was — spread across my kitchen table.

More money than I'd ever made in one place.

Not from a paycheck.
Not from luck.

But because strangers believed enough to pull out their credit cards and mail them to my home address.

I stood there staring at the table, realizing that this wasn't a side project anymore.

This was a business.

* * *

The next day, it happened again.

Just like *Groundhog Day* the movie!

Another yellow slip in my mailbox.
Another drive to the post office.
Another stack of subscription cards waiting behind the counter.

Then it kept repeating — day after day.

* * *

But the piles were getting bigger.

The second day: 769.
The third day: 951.
The fourth day: 1,110.
By the fifth day: 1,432.

I started keeping track because I almost didn't believe it myself.

By the end of the first week, I had received 4,785 subscription cards.

They kept coming in daily, faster than I could process them — each one filled out by someone I had never met, each one mailed to my home address.

* * *

By the end of that month, the total was well over a thousand subscriptions — most at $119 each, many international at $149.

Developers from around the world were signing up.

Trusting a magazine that hadn't even printed its first issue yet.

I wasn't chasing the business anymore.

It was chasing me.

Ladies and gentlemen, in the span of about a month, I had become a paper millionaire — on paper only — thanks to the trust of *Powersoft* chairman Mitchell Kertzman.

I couldn't help myself.

I loaded every subscription card into my beat-up Honda Civic and drove them to work like they were a trophy. I showed them to anyone who would look, joking that there was a million dollars sitting in my trunk.

It was absurd.

And I knew it.

But I also knew what it meant.
That was the same day Carmen quit her accounting job and moved into my Jersey City townhouse to work out of my home office full time.

At that point, this wasn't just momentum anymore.

It was commitment.

CHAPTER 6

I already had more than one million dollars'
worth of subscription cards waiting to be
processed."

A Million Dollars I Couldn't Touch

Two months after announcing *PowerBuilder Developer's Journal* on the *Powersoft* BBS, I found myself staring at more than one million dollars' worth of subscription cards spread across my kitchen table.

It was exhilarating — and terrifying.

I had a serious problem.

I didn't have a credit card merchant account. In fact, I didn't even have a business checking account.

* * *

At the same time, the artwork for the ads I had sold began arriving in the mail, each envelope stuffed with prepaid checks.

Altogether, they totaled about $18,000 — enough to cover the printing cost of 10,000 copies of my first issue, with money left over.

There was just one catch.

I had told advertisers our company name was *SYS-CON Publications*, and that's exactly how they had written the checks.

* * *

I walked to several banks near my home, checks in hand, confident this would be a formality. Every one of them gave me the same answer. They couldn't open a business checking account because my company wasn't incorporated. Apparently, being a "business" wasn't enough.

I wasn't IBM — but that didn't seem to matter.

* * *

So I went back to the most powerful tool of the early 1990s — the Yellow Pages.

I found a number that felt almost too convenient to be real:

1-800-COMPANY.

I called Company Corporation, read my credit card number over the phone, and just like that, they incorporated me as SYS-CON Publications, Inc.

Less than a week later, a thick corporate book arrived at my door.

Inside were the articles of incorporation, a corporate seal, and every official document that suddenly made my kitchen-table operation a real company.

It still wasn't enough. No bank would open a business checking account for me — never mind a merchant account to process subscriptions. The explanation was always the same. The business was home-based.

And to the banks, that meant it wasn't a "real" business — regardless of the checks piling up on my kitchen table.

* * *

Eventually, I found a bank at the corner of 45th Street and Third Avenue in Manhattan that didn't flinch.

I was greeted with a smile and assured that I would walk out in under an

hour with both a business checking account and a merchant account —
checkbook included.

It was Habib Bank, a Pakistani bank.

My checks would say *Habib Bank*, not Chase or Citibank.

It wasn't the image I had imagined, but at that point, image mattered far
less than survival.

With a business checking account finally open, I wasted no time deposit-
ing the $18,000 in advertising checks that had been sitting on my kitchen
table. For the first time in weeks, I could breathe. And sleep. The printing
bill was covered.

I could finally focus on laying out the first issue upstairs, sitting on the
edge of my bed, turning my bedroom into a production studio.

* * *

Soon after, a Habib Bank employee arrived with a credit card terminal
and a quick lesson on how to use it.

I explained that I already had more than one million dollars' worth of
subscription cards waiting to be processed.

That's when I hit the real showstopper.

* * *

My merchant account allowed me to process no more than $20,000 per
month.

Home-based business.
Fraud risk.
No credit history.

The rules were simple.

Prove yourself first.

If there were no *chargebacks* or refund requests, the limit would be raised — slowly.

As I began entering subscriptions into a makeshift Excel spreadsheet, preparing to merge them into a Word Avery label template, Carmen moved with remarkable speed, processing our first $20,000 worth of subscriptions.

By the end of that initial push, we had roughly $38,000 in the bank — about $83,000 in today's money — a number that felt both surreal and fragile.

It was obvious we needed help.

I called several temporary employment agencies, hoping to bring in someone part-time.

Every conversation ended the same way.

The moment I mentioned that the business was home-based, they shut the door.

Sorry — we can't help you.

Another dead end.

In the first issue of PBDJ

I announced a bestseller book

And a world tour

Before either existed

A Bestseller and a World Tour

In February 1994, I began laying out the first issue of my very first magazine using Aldus PageMaker on my Macintosh Classic, balanced on the edge of my bed in my Jersey City townhouse.

I included two full-page house ads — my own ads. The premiere issue of *PowerBuilder Developer's Journal* was scheduled to debut at the Powersoft User Conference in Disney World that June.

The first full-page ad announced a book:

PowerBuilder 4.0: Secrets of the Masters
by Steve Benfield

The second full-page ad promoted something even bigger:
World Tour with PBDJ — 10 Cities in 30 Days.

It was a two-day conference series scheduled to travel through Los Angeles, San Francisco, Toronto, Austin, Chicago, New York City, Boston, Washington, D.C., Atlanta, and Philadelphia.

As for the world tour, I had solid dates — and nothing else.
But once the dates were printed, the ad looked real.

And somehow, that made it real.

At the time, I had never seen the advice later attributed to Richard Branson:

"If somebody offers you an amazing opportunity but you are not sure you can do it, say yes — then learn how to do it later."

Without realizing it, I was already living by that rule.

* * *

Over the next five months, I finished designing the first issue. It was more or less printable.

I paid the Brooklyn printer and received the magazines just five days before the Orlando conference. I brought 5,000 copies with me.

After landing, I drove my rental car to the Orlando airport cargo terminal. It took three trips to haul all the boxes to the Dolphin Hotel.

When I finally arrived, nearly 100 delegates surrounded my car. They ripped open the boxes, each grabbing as many copies as they could carry, and walked away reading my premiere issue as they went.

David Litwack was there. He grabbed a copy.

Steve and I then took the elevator up to Mitchell Kertzman's room, where he posed for a photo holding *PowerBuilder Developer's Journal* in his hand.

* * *

There was just one problem.

I had forgotten to mention the book to Steve Benfield.

He discovered he was writing one when he saw the magazine in Orlando, surrounded by 5,000 PowerBuilder developers at the Powersoft User Conference.

He came up to me and said,

"I just saw it in the magazine. I guess I'm writing a book. Let me jump on it right away."

* * *

That book would become a huge hit.

I found a printer in Secaucus, New Jersey, and printed 10,000 copies. Jim laid out nearly 600 pages using PageMaker.

We priced the book at $69.99 but sold it for $40, plus shipping and handling. The printing cost was one dollar per copy.

Over the next twelve months, the book generated roughly $250,000 in profit.

I offered the authors either 5 percent equity in the company or $50 cash per article.

Every one of them chose cash — including Steve.

Twenty years later, he still calls me from time to time and asks if he can finally collect his 5 percent of SYS-CON Media.

* * *

My 10-City World Tour with PBDJ was actually my first live event — though I didn't realize it at the time. I simply announced it without overthinking what I was doing.

To me, it felt like a natural extension of the magazine.

If companies were willing to advertise in it, I also needed things to sell to my readers. A book and a live event were the two most obvious products I could create."

I reviewed the dates I had placed in the ad. The first two cities were Los Angeles and San Francisco.

It was time to repeat the same formula I had used to finance the magazine's first issue.

I began selling world tour tickets, sponsorships, and exhibition space — and it worked immediately.

My print advertisers became sponsors and exhibitors. The authors from the premiere issue became the speakers. And my readers became paying attendees, eager to learn PowerBuilder directly from the celebrity PBDJ writers they had been following.

I secured hotel space in each city. Knowing I would still need operational help, I hired J.R. Shuman Associates — the same team that produced the official Powersoft User Conference.

* * *

The 10-city world tour turned out to be extremely profitable.

Even more profitable than the book.

* * *

Within twelve months of bringing my premiere issue to that user conference, I was no longer experimenting.

I was a real company — generating real revenue.

All in under a year.

CHAPTER 8

Dinner in Paris

One conversation

One unexpected connection

And everything changed.

My First Date With Carmen

Over time, the credit card merchant account restrictions began to ease. Our initial processing limit of $20,000 per month gradually increased, and after eight months with zero chargebacks, the bank finally granted us full approval to process all of our subscription orders.

* * *

Then one afternoon, I logged into the account and froze.

The balance had crossed one million dollars.

I was officially a millionaire in less than a year.

* * *

Of course, not all of that was earned income under accrual accounting rules. We were recognizing only one-twelfth of the subscription revenue each time a new issue was delivered to subscribers.

Still, I was staring at a bank statement that showed seven figures.

And it felt very real.

That moment called for a celebration. We hadn't taken any real time off for months.

I came in from the post office, walked upstairs, and said, "Carmen, tomorrow is Friday. I'm taking you out to dinner. Bring a small bag —

and don't forget your passport."

* * *

By noon the next day, we were in a cab headed to JFK, boarding a flight to Paris.

Saturday night, we had dinner near the Eiffel Tower. Sunday was spent sightseeing. By Monday morning, we were back at work.

* * *

I still travel that way.

Just before Christmas this year, Marilyn and I flew to Zurich and London. We had breakfast at Claridge's, bought organic CackleBean eggs in the basement of Harrods, and flew back home.

A weekend.

Then Monday came again.

CHAPTER 9

We were fast
Very fast
Like a race car driver
With no brakes

Fast. Very Fast.

I was at Jim's garage production space. We were getting ready to send the second issue of *PBDJ* to the printer. Jim had taken over the design and layout from me after my experimental premiere issue — which I had produced alone in my bedroom and which took nearly six months to complete.

As we were wrapping up, Jim realized he needed to fill half a page with a house ad.

We stood there staring at the empty space, trying to decide what to put in it.

Then the phone rang.

It was Ted Coombs — one of our writers.

He said, "Fuat, I can't believe you're not publishing a magazine about Java. It's going to be huge. Revolutionary. You have to publish a Java magazine."

I didn't hesitate.

"Ted, we will," I said. "You're the editor-in-chief of *Java Developer's Journal*. Could you send Jim your editorial column when you get a chance? And feel free to accept articles from authoritative names. We won't publish anything without your approval."

Ted said sure.

We hung up.

I turned to Jim and said, "That half page you have open — let's use it to announce *Java Developer's Journal*. Branding, logo, and a mock cover."

Jim nodded and went straight to work.

* * *

We announced JDJ in the second issue of *PBDJ* — at least a year before most technology publishers had even heard the word Java.

Yes.

We were fast.

Very fast.

CHAPTER 10

PowerBuilder in one hand
Java in the other
Two new magazines
One big bet.

Six Months, Two Magazines

I f *PowerBuilder Developer's Journal* made us a real publisher, *Java Developer's Journal* became our first big wave. It put us on the map and established us as a serious player in the technology media world.

* * *

After announcing *Java Developer's Journal* with a house ad in the second issue of *PBDJ*, the response was immediate. Once the magazine reached our readers, I could see real traction building around *JDJ*.

My formula was working.

We sold advertising pages and subscriptions first, generating enough revenue to fund the printing of the premiere issue.

* * *

Around the same time, I secured a magazine distributor located just down the street from our offices that agreed to carry both publications. They gave us national and international placement for *PBDJ* and *Java Developer's Journal*, putting them on the shelves at Borders, Barnes & Noble, independent U.S. newsstands, and key retailers worldwide.

Curtis Circulation Company, based in New Milford, New Jersey, became our national magazine distributor throughout the 1990s. At the time, Curtis was one of the largest single-copy magazine distributors in the United States, responsible for getting publications onto newsstands, bookstores, and retail outlets nationwide. They handled logistics, retail placement, sales reporting, and returns — serving as the critical link between publishers and the national newsstand market during the peak era of print magazines.

* * *

With a 30–40 percent sell-through rate, newsstand distribution was not a cost center. It didn't generate meaningful profit either — but that wasn't the point.

What mattered was visibility.

Being on major newsstands dramatically strengthened our credibility and allowed us to command higher advertising page rates.

* * *

To further reinforce our media kit, we became members of both BPA and ABC, the two leading magazine circulation audit bureaus.

Java Developer's Journal circulation numbers were officially audited.

That single step gave us a decisive competitive advantage.

If any other publisher wanted to enter the Java space, they would be going up against verified numbers — not promises, projections, or hype.

And that made all the difference.

* * *

Within twelve months of publishing my very first issue, I was now running two magazine titles, each generating both advertising and subscription revenue. Cash flow stayed positive at all times.

Every Friday, Joan would walk into my office with her cash flow report. Before even looking at the numbers, I could accurately guess our cash position in the bank. I was monitoring the pulse of the business around the clock. I didn't need to see the report to know where we stood.

* * *

That same first year, I also brought in serious revenue from the book and from twelve city events.

What began as an accident had turned into a proven formula. Throughout the twenty years I ran my media business, I never needed a loan.

I never quite understood why people launched new companies using borrowed money — whether from banks or investors — when it was possible to build momentum first and scale from revenue.

The only money I used in the beginning came from my own credit card. Renting a car to drive to Boston. Printing subscription cards to include in product packaging. Buying postage stamps for my first media kits.

All of it added up to about $1,200 on a completely maxed-out card. If you have a real business, it should be profitable from the first day.

* * *

I still carry that same card today. I've had it since 1984.

Chase should probably invite me into one of their commercials.

* * *

Then the money started coming in.

And it paid the bills.

CHAPTER 11

Riding the Java wave
Two booth workers
One crowded expo
And miracles everywhere

Riding The Java Wave

S cott McNealy's Sun Microsystems didn't collapse because it lacked innovation. It collapsed because the industry moved faster than its business model.

Sun built some of the most advanced technology of its era — Solaris, SPARC, and Java — yet remained dependent on selling expensive hardware just as the world shifted toward cheap servers, open-source software, and eventually cloud computing. While others turned Sun's ideas into scalable businesses, Sun struggled to monetize its own brilliance.

* * *

In the end, being early wasn't enough.

In technology, timing and execution matter as much as vision.

* * *

As cloud computing eventually became the end of Sun Microsystems, it became our next beginning. We moved from Java to cloud seamlessly — years ahead of most of the industry. While others hesitated or waited to see how the market would evolve, we committed early. Many competitors never even attempted to challenge us and chose to remain on the sidelines.

Our CloudEXPO conferences would go on to dominate the cloud media space for decades.

But at the time, Java was everything.

Our premiere issue of *Java Developer's Journal* was ready to go to print even before Sun had fully organized its first user conference, JavaOne.

Just thirty days before JavaOne was scheduled to take place at the Moscone Center in San Francisco, Oracle was preparing for its own annual event — Oracle OpenWorld — at the very same venue.

We were media sponsors of both conferences.

* * *

We placed full-page ads announcing JavaOne and Oracle OpenWorld, then sent the issue to the printer.

I emailed Larry Ellison personally, explaining that *Java Developer's Journal* was one of Oracle's media sponsors. We wanted to officially launch the magazine at his event and requested booth space so we could distribute our premiere issue to attendees. Roughly 10,000 delegates were expected.

His reply came back almost immediately, with several Oracle executives copied.

"It's a lovely idea."

* * *

From that moment on, we received full cooperation from Oracle's public relations team. Throughout the event, members of the expo staff kept rushing up to me, smiling, and saying, "Larry said it's a lovely idea."

That week, we got exactly the exposure we had hoped for.

* * *

As Oracle OpenWorld wrapped up, we turned our full attention to what came next — the very first JavaOne.

Java had been officially introduced earlier that year. On May 23, 1995, Sun Microsystems unveiled Java at the SunWorld conference.

The announcement ignited rapid global adoption. Within months, Java was everywhere — and *Java Developer's Journal* suddenly found itself riding at the center of one of the fastest technology waves the industry had ever seen.

By then, we knew it.

Java was our big wave.

We had to focus on our newborn baby at full intensity.

For JavaOne, I went all in.

I hired two forty-foot-long billboard trucks, each wrapped with massive, backlit graphics — not only on the sides, but on the rear panels as well, so cars following behind couldn't miss them.

When the JavaOne conference opened the following month, those trucks circled the Moscone Center nonstop.

Not a single attendee could miss our giant magazine cover announcing *Java Developer's Journal* at the first-ever JavaOne — an event that stunned the industry by drawing more than 20,000 participants and selling out the entire expo floor.

* * *

We ordered 1,000 T-shirts and 1,000 coffee mugs from China at one dollar each. We placed mugs on nearly every booth across the show floor.

At our own booth, I stacked 5,000 copies of the magazine.

From a distance, all you could see was a mountain of JDJs.

The night before the show, we stopped for a couple of drinks at a local gentlemen's club on the way back to the hotel. On impulse, I hired two of the dancers to help work our booth the next day.

When the expo floor opened that morning, they showed up.

We immediately realized we had a problem.

They were dressed exactly as they had been the night before — which is to say, barely dressed at all.

* * *

We scrambled to cover them as much as we could, then I sent them out with instructions to walk the floor and collect business cards from exhibitors.

Less than an hour later, they were back.

There were more than a thousand exhibitors at JavaOne.

* * *

I said, "Ladies, we want the business cards of the marketing managers. Why are you back so fast?"

They looked at me and said, "We didn't miss a single booth."

They weren't exaggerating.

They had collected more than a thousand business cards — from nearly every company on the expo floor.

Those cards became our A-list advertising leads for the next issue.

Almost immediately after they started working the booth, my Motorola flip phone rang.

It was Carmen.

"I hear you hired hookers as booth bimbos," she said. Advertisers had been calling her all day, reporting that we had dancers working our booth.

When she learned what those two almost-naked college girls had actually accomplished, she paused.

Then she calmed down.

* * *

I paid the girls, thanked them for their help, and asked them not to return the next day.

They had done their job.

Results, after all, tend to speak for themselves.

Our presence at JavaOne was intimidating — at least to our competitors.

The other Java magazine, *Java Report*, published by Rick Friedman of Siggs Publications, was clearly rattled when I ran into him on the floor.

He yelled, "Java Developer's Journal is everywhere! I go to the bathroom and see copies stacked on the counter. What are you doing? And what are those monster trucks circling the city?"

* * *

Not long after that conference, Rick sold his company and retired.

I hired two of his senior managers — Larry and Miles.

CHAPTER 12

A man in a kilt arrived
No appointment
No explanation
And no intention of
leaving.

The Man in the Kilt

We were in our Pearl River, New York office — 39 East Central Avenue — the building I bought from the pizza man because he'd been annoying us since the day we moved in.

I hadn't driven home to Jersey City in about six months. Instead, I was crashing at the office, sleeping under the conference room table. At some point, the place stopped feeling like work and started feeling like home — part office, part apartment, part psychological experiment.

After hours, the office became my living room. I walked around barefoot like I paid rent. My beard and hair were five months overdue for a barber visit — and honestly, that felt optimistic. My jeans barely zipped anymore, and when they did, it was a negotiation.

We still had a few hundred leftover T-shirts from the last show. I grabbed a clean one and pulled it over my head. They were all the same color — generic giveaway stock — with STAFF printed across the back.

Which was perfect.

Because at that point, I didn't look like the founder.

I looked like the first homeless man you'd cross the street to avoid if you saw me coming.

One day, while moving between offices, I noticed a man wearing a kilt — the full ethnic outfit. I stopped and asked Robert who he was.

Robert said, "He told us he's from Scotland. He's a Java developer. He's in love with *Java Developer's Journal*. He wanted to meet the team behind the magazine."

Then he added, almost casually, "He's been asking Jim questions for the last hour."

My conference-room bedroom at night doubled as our SYS-CON Radio studio during the day.

Robert's college friend, Chad Sidler, wanted to become a radio personality when he grew up. So Robert gave him a chair and a microphone — and that was that. Chad went live from the conference room every day. He had a great radio voice too. Deep. Confident. Professional. I was pretty sure he was just reading articles from our own journals, but on the air it sounded like breaking news.

After a few days, I noticed Alan Williamson acting strange. He moved carefully around the office, always trying to impress Chad.

Eventually, once he felt comfortable enough, Alan pulled Carmen aside and whispered,

"Who's the homeless man? He's scary-looking. I've been avoiding him since I arrived."

Carmen didn't miss a beat.

"That's Fuat," she said. "He's the owner."

Alan froze.

The problem was that Chad was taller than everyone else, sitting behind a microphone, speaking in that deep bass radio voice. So Alan naturally assumed *he* was the boss — and had been kissing his ass nonstop since day one.

After that very awkward introduction, Alan became one of the key members of our team. He went on to play a major role in the global success of both *Java Developer's Journal* and *Linux World Magazine*. In fact, Alan produced the very first issues of *Linux World* — long before anyone imagined how big it would become.

Years later, Carmen practically adopted Alan and gave him one of the bedrooms in my Upper Saddle River mansion. Once, while we were having drinks, he casually announced that all three of his children had been conceived in that house.

Shortly after our meeting, we named him editor-in-chief of *Java Developer's Journal*. With the content he put together, JDJ's monthly audited circulation quickly exceeded 200,000 copies — serious, targeted reach for our advertisers.

At the time, I was publishing twelve monthly magazines, all carried by Barnes & Noble and on newsstands worldwide.

For *Java Developer's Journal*, Carmen and her six sales managers consistently generated more than $1 million per issue in advertising revenue for nearly two decades.

The first time she walked into my office and said, "This month JDJ's ad revenue is one million dollars," I didn't believe her.

I asked Joan to audit the numbers — and told Carmen that if they were correct, I'd take her entire department to Hawaii.

They were.

So I did.

CHAPTER 13

We started publishing magazines
in French, Korean, and Chinese.

From Allaire to Adobe Six More Titles

After successfully delivering *PowerBuilder Developer's Journal* to Powersoft customers — and then accidentally launching *Java Developer's Journal* just six months later — we were always on the lookout for the next opportunity.

* * *

I honestly don't remember exactly how *ColdFusion Developer's Journal* came to fruition. What I do remember is walking past Robert's desk one day and saying, "Robert, congratulations. You're the editor of CFDJ. Please gather the content for the first issue and put it together with Alex."

And just like that, we launched *ColdFusion Developer's Journal*.

From its very first issue, CFDJ quickly became popular among ColdFusion developers and profitable for us as well. During that period, we also published several ColdFusion-related books.

* * *

Ben Forta, one of the most recognized names in the ColdFusion community, became a regular columnist for the magazine. We even achieved a record sell-through rate on newsstands — further proof that this accidental formula kept working.

* * *

After Macromedia acquired Allaire, we became the go-to magazine publisher for Macromedia's developer community with our flagship title, *MX Developer's Journal*. At its peak, we published *MX Developer's Journal* in four additional languages — French, Korean, Mandarin, and Cantonese Chinese.

CHAPTER 14

Everyone had a stock tip.

No one cared about profits.

Then the bubble burst.

Irrational Exuberance

The late 1990s didn't feel like a boom — they felt like permission. Permission to believe that gravity no longer applied, that losses were temporary, and that every idea with a dot-com at the end was destined to change the world. Money appeared faster than logic, valuations outran reality, and optimism became a substitute for discipline. We didn't think we were being reckless. We thought we were being visionary. And for a brief, intoxicating moment, everyone was right — until suddenly, no one was.

* * *

Everyone who walked into my office had a stock tip and a success story.

David, the printer across the street, bragged that his AOL shares had doubled overnight. Alex, my graphic designer, couldn't stop talking about Apple. It felt like nobody was actually working anymore — they were all trading. The market wasn't something people invested in. It was something they lived inside.

At the center of that frenzy stood Harvey Houtkin, widely known as the father of modern day trading — the man who put Wall Street on a computer screen and convinced an entire generation that speed could replace experience. The markets felt alive then: flashing, addictive, unforgiving. People weren't just trading stocks. They were trading hope, fear, and ego.

When I sold my Pearl River building to Harvey, it felt strangely symbolic. Two people shaped by the same electric moment — a time when belief moved faster than reason, and everyone thought the ride would never end.

* * *

Harvey explained his trading revolution to me with complete conviction.

I didn't have time for it. I was running a real business. I had payroll, printing deadlines, advertisers, and twenty-hour days. Day trading felt like noise.

Still, something pulled at me.

* * *

One afternoon, I went to my bank branch, requested a two-million-dollar cashier's check, and drove straight to the Fidelity Investments office on Route 17.

I walked in, waited in line, and when it was my turn, I told the woman behind the counter that I wanted to open a trading account.

She said, "You need fifty dollars to open an account."

I told her I had brought a bank check.

She entered my name, Social Security number, address, and phone number into her computer. Then I slid the check across the counter.

She stared at it.

Then she looked back at me and said,

"There are too many zeros on this check."

Before I could respond, she pressed the panic button beneath the counter.

I stood there quietly, watching her expression shift from confusion to concern. A security guard appeared from the back office. Then another employee. No one spoke. They just watched.

Across the street sat the Mercedes dealership — the same place where, not long before, a salesman had looked past me as if I didn't belong.

In that moment, something became clear.

In the era of irrational exuberance, money moved faster than trust — and credibility lagged far behind both.

Less than six months later, the dot-com bubble burst.

My two-million-dollar trading account vanished with it.

I carried those losses forward on my tax returns for nearly twenty years — a long, quiet reminder of a time when confidence outran caution, and even smart people confused momentum for permanence.

"I knew Jack Kennedy. Jack Kennedy was a friend of mine. Senator, you're no Jack Kennedy."

That line, delivered by Lloyd Bentsen during the 1988 vice-presidential debate, stayed with me for years — not because it was political, but because it captured a universal truth.

Experience cannot be imitated.

I knew artificial intelligence. I taught AI at CloudEXPO to engineers from Google, Facebook, and Twitter in 2013 — long before it became a headline, a stock symbol, or a gold rush.

And just like the dot-com era before it, I can feel it again.

The next bubble is forming.

And when it breaks, it may be far worse.

CHAPTER 15

The day I met Roger Strukhoff and Jeremy Geelan

Roger and Jeremy

My childhood friend — my roommate — and I were extremely lonely.

Not Netflix-and-chill lonely.

More like two fish in a tank at a dentist's office, watching life happen on the other side of the glass.

We had no social life.

None.

Zero.

Even our shadows had stopped following us.

This was before GPS.

Before smartphones.

Before MapQuest.

Back then, getting lost was a lifestyle choice.

All we knew was that somewhere in New Jersey there was a Turkish community.

Supposedly in Paterson.

For several weekends, we tried to find it.

Every time, we failed.

We'd drive around, get lost, and somehow end up in the Spanish part of the city.

Wrong language.

Wrong signs.

Wrong food.

We'd look at each other thinking, *this can't be Turkey... but the music is good*, then drive home in silence.

* * *

Finally, one Sunday — with slightly better directions and dangerously high optimism — we found it.

The Turkish community was concentrated along Main Street in South Paterson.

I parked my beat-up Honda Civic in front of a tiny hole-in-the-wall place called *Çiçek Video*.

Inside, a guy was renting bootleg Turkish VHS tapes — two-month-old news from Turkey, pirated movies, and enough nostalgia to trigger instant homesickness.

We rented a few tapes and crossed the street to the Turkish butcher.

Now, I should explain something.

I have a big mouth.

Always have.

Silence makes me uncomfortable, so I fill it with words — usually the wrong ones.

I said,

"We've been looking for the Turkish neighborhood for weeks. We finally found it. We're roommates. We don't know anyone in America. It's time we meet a nice Turkish girl and get married."

* * *

The butcher didn't say a word.
He simply vanished into the back.

A minute later, he returned carrying half a lamb — legs, chops, everything — and handed it to us like we'd just won the grand prize on a daytime game show.

Then he waved his hand and refused to take any money.

We walked out holding a dead animal, trying to understand which part of the conversation had gone wrong.

Before leaving, I went back into the video store and explained what had just happened.

A few Turks immediately started laughing.

One guy laughed so hard he had to sit down, like he'd been waiting his whole life for this exact story.

Finally, the owner said,

"He has six daughters at home. He thought you came to ask for one of them."

We got free lamb.
No phone numbers.
No daughters.

But still — it felt like progress.

Traumatized, embarrassed, and suddenly responsible for a large amount of meat, we avoided Paterson for a while.

It felt safer that way.

* * *

Not long after, my roommate discovered another Turkish community — this one upstate in a small town called Chestnut Ridge, right on the New York–New Jersey border.

Close enough to feel familiar.

Far enough to pretend the lamb incident never happened.

He asked if I could drive him there.

* * *

Every Saturday night, they held social gatherings.

One family would cook for the entire group in a restaurant-sized kitchen.

The community revolved around a Turkish mosque, with many families living right on the property.

It was organized, warm, welcoming — and best of all, nobody tried to give us livestock.

* * *

We found the place, and I dropped him off.

He said,
"Come back and pick me up around midnight."

Midnight.
Perfect.

Just enough time for me to feel productive while doing absolutely nothing.

* * *

I drove to the nearest movie theater at the Spring Valley Marketplace and watched a movie I barely remember.

I ate popcorn and wondered whether my roommate was meeting the love of his life — or being offered another free animal, possibly larger.

When the movie ended, I picked him up and we drove back to Jersey City.

The trip took an hour to an hour and a half, depending on traffic and how much time I spent thinking about how strange immigrant life could feel.

* * *

We were grown men.
Employed.
Living in America.

Yet our weekends were spent driving long distances just to hear our own language and feel normal for a few hours.

Looking back, it was awkward, lonely, and slightly ridiculous.

At the time, though, it felt like progress.

My roommate knew exactly what was going on in my life.

I was working a full-time job while trying to launch a magazine, sell ads, design layouts, and figure out how I was going to fulfill subscriptions I had no idea how to deliver.

Somehow, he turned my stress into a sales pitch.

Apparently, he told the community about the "serious business opportunity" I had fallen into — and how it desperately needed help.

The community was led by a highly respected, scholarly older man.

When he heard my story, he didn't hesitate.

* * *

He told my roommate,

"Tell your roommate to rent the mosque's standalone garage on the street and move out of his apartment. It's fully finished — heat, air conditioning, everything. A perfect office."

Then he added,

"He also has a full staff here. Let him meet Jim Morgan."

* * *

Jim — whose Turkish name was Jamal — was an accomplished graphic designer and the son of a rabbi.

At the time, I thought I was barely surviving.

I didn't yet realize I had just been handed office space, staff, and a professional designer — courtesy of a mosque garage.

The move took planning. The phone was already ringing nonstop at my townhouse in Jersey City. Carmen had practically moved in and was working twelve-hour days out of my living room. My home had quietly become a call center with furniture.

I paid $500 a month for the garage office, and Jim set up his Mac there.

We even installed a phone line — this was before cell phones, back when wires still mattered.

When the phone rang, we answered confidently,

"SYS-CON Production. How may I help you?"

It sounded so official we almost believed it ourselves.

* * *

Fast forward twelve months.
We had published six issues.

I produced the first one myself in my bedroom, surrounded by coffee cups and panic.

By the second issue, Jim Morgan had taken over the layout — and thankfully never gave it back.

About a year later, the garage door opened and a tall, confident guy walked in, as if wandering into random garages was part of his daily routine.

He stuck out his hand and said,

"Hi, I'm Roger Strukhoff. I live in California. I publish *Sybase Magazine*. I do custom publishing. Companies pay me, I produce the magazine, and I mail it to their readers."

I nodded like this made perfect sense — two professionals meeting in a converted garage in New Jersey.

I said,
"Nice to meet you, Roger. This is Jim Morgan, our art director and vice president of production."

At that point, we were still adjusting to the idea that people from California even knew we existed — let alone treated us like a real company.

* * *

After some small talk, Roger got serious.

He explained that he had been publishing *Sybase Magazine* as a custom title.

Sybase paid him to produce it.

But then Sybase acquired Powersoft — and suddenly everything changed.

* * *

"They're telling me," he said, "that there's a publisher in New Jersey producing a monthly magazine called *PowerBuilder Developer's Journal*. A well-respected publication."

He paused.

"And it's not costing them a dime."
He looked straight at me.
"And that publisher," he said, "is you."

* * *

That's how I met Roger Strukhoff.

In hindsight, he was the first friendly competitor we ever encountered — though we didn't know we were competitors yet.

As SYS-CON gained traction, the industry around us began to shift.

A few rival publications disappeared along the way — some we knew about, others we discovered only in hindsight, long after they were already gone.

By then, the garage phase of the company was behind us.

We made a deliberate decision to bring sales, accounting, customer service, editorial, and production under one roof.

In theory, we were becoming a real company.

* * *

We found a building in Pearl River, New York, at 39 East Central Avenue.

Our offices were on the second floor, above three street-level businesses: an antique shop, a barber, and a bagel store.

The space was in rough shape — worse than the bootleg video store in Paterson, which I had once believed set the absolute bottom for commercial real estate.

* * *

The building was owned by an immigrant pizza man and his wife.

They treated ownership like an open-door policy.

They showed up unannounced, wandered the halls, and occasionally picked arguments with random employees, as if workplace tension were included in the rent.

Eventually, I'd had enough.

I called their realtor, Steve Bernasconi, and asked whether the owner would consider selling the building.

Steve called back with a number.
I wrote a check and became a landlord overnight.

That's when I learned another lesson of entrepreneurship: solving one problem often creates a more expensive version of it.

Suddenly, tenants were calling me to change light bulbs and unclog toilets.

This was not the kind of vertical integration I had in mind.

* * *

So I handed the keys — and the headaches — to Abraham, one of our designers who also happened to be handy with home remodeling, and put him in charge of managing our three ground-floor tenants. That freed me up to get back to the business I actually knew how to run. By then, our editorial operation had its own structure. M'lou Pinkham was our senior editor. She reported to Jim Morgan, but she ran editorial hiring independently. Writers, copy editors, freelancers — if they passed through the door, M'lou had brought them in.

* * *

That's when I first noticed Jeremy.

He was sitting in production next to the printer on what could generously be described as a chair.

It had no back.
One arm was missing.

And it looked like it had already lived a long and difficult life before arriving at our office.

* * *

I asked Alex and Robert who the new guy was. "M'lou hired him," they said. "We think he's a copy editor." I noticed the accent immediately. It stood out in a room full of New Jersey voices.

"Where's he from?" I asked.

They looked at me like I'd just violated an HR policy that didn't exist yet.

"You can't ask that."

I listened to him talk for a moment.

Whatever his title was, I thought, that accent is doing half the work already.

I didn't know what we were going to do with him yet — but I knew we were going to do something.

CHAPTER 16

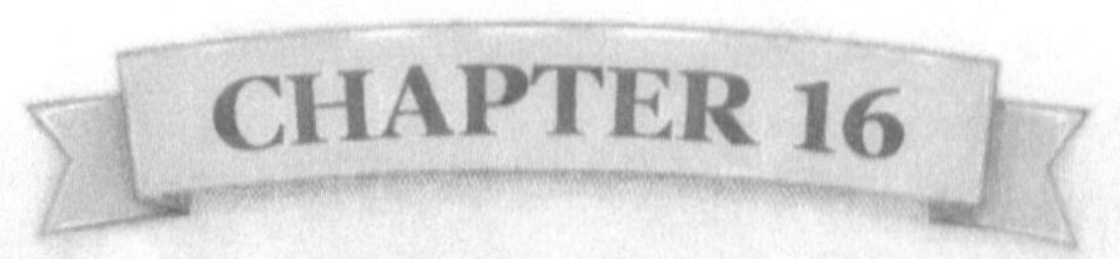

We became the TMZ of Silicon Valley

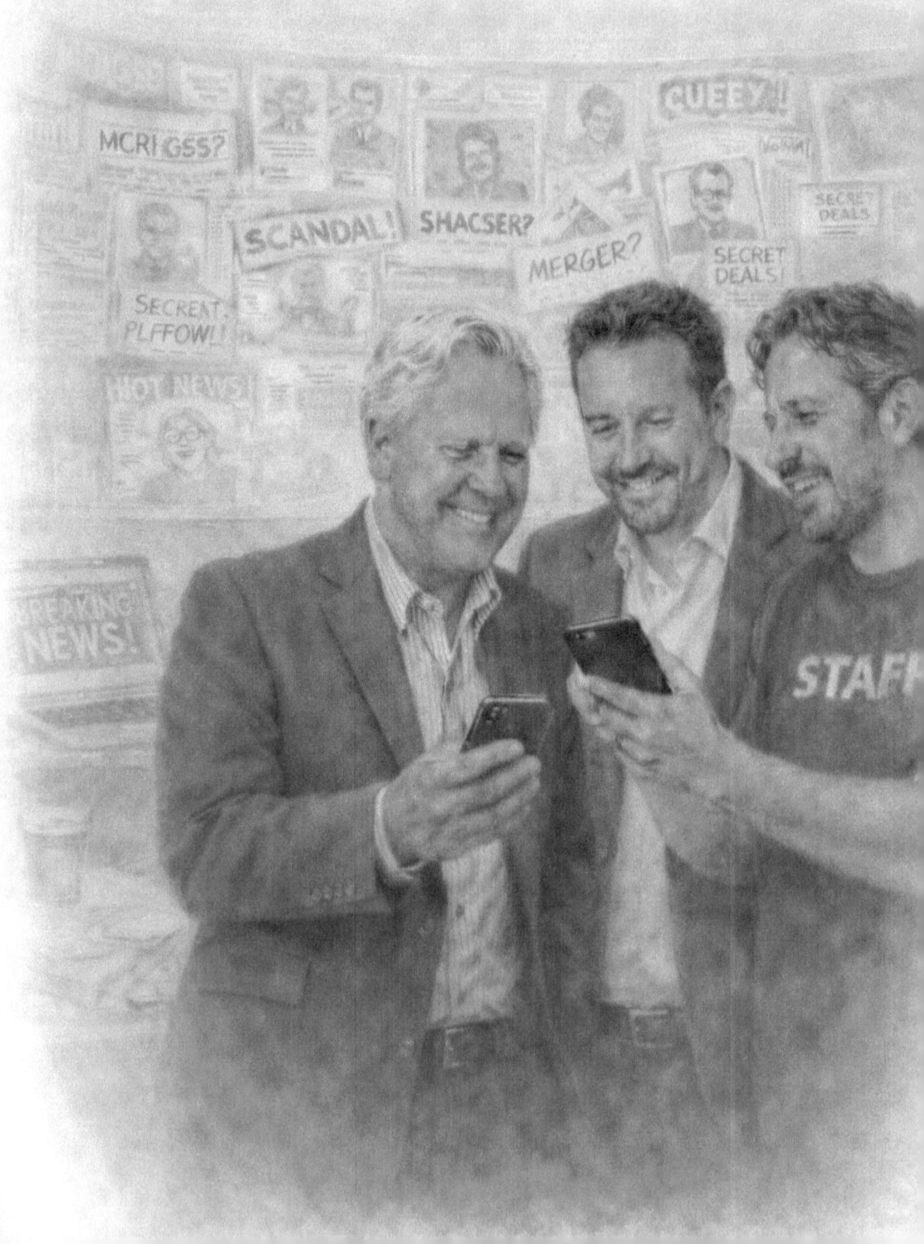

The TMZ of Tech

R ick Ross, the founder of Java Lobby, called me one day and said, "I want to introduce you to Maureen O'Gara. I think she should write for you."

I told him I'd drive out and meet her.

I had never heard her name before.

* * *

That week, I drove to Long Island and walked into Maureen's office.

After that first meeting, we started publishing her weekly newsletter on our Linux site, *Linux Business News*. Almost immediately, it took off.

Only then did I understand who she really was.

Maureen wasn't just a reporter.

She was wired directly into Silicon Valley.

She was on a first-name basis with Bill Gates, Steve Jobs, Larry Ellison—people most journalists only saw from a distance.

She broke stories aggressively and fast, and she didn't worry much about who she offended along the way.

Together, we became something like the *TMZ* of technology.

Around that time, we licensed the *LinuxWorld* brand from IDG. Pat McGovern ran the *LinuxWorld* conferences but didn't have a print publication. He sent Colin Crawford from California to negotiate the deal.

Colin was IDG's vice president of new business development and operations, and before that, he'd been president and CEO of Mac Publishing, the publisher of *Macworld* magazine.

* * *

Colin came to our Montvale, New Jersey, office with a one-page acquisition offer from IDG to buy SYS-CON Media.

Instead of selling, we ended up licensing the *LinuxWorld* name and launching the magazine in both print and online formats.

We paid IDG ten percent of top-line revenue.

LinuxWorld quickly became the most widely distributed Linux magazine in the world.

That was the only meeting I ever had with Colin Crawford.

I used to visit Maureen regularly.

We'd meet early in the morning, grab breakfast at the diner next door to her office, and then I'd drive back to New Jersey.

One morning, I walked into her office and saw a man asleep on her brown leather sofa.

* * *

He slowly got up, washed his face, opened a fresh package with a white shirt inside, put it on, tied his tie, and joined us for breakfast.

"This is Ken Crone," Maureen said casually. "Interim CEO of Computer Associates. He's in the middle of a divorce. His wife has the twelve-bedroom mansion, so he's crashing here."

We didn't talk business over eggs.

* * *

Ken was extremely sharp.

He had come from the publishing world and had single-handedly structured CMP Media's $920 million sale to United News & Media.

Despite that, he told me he never received a single dollar for his efforts.

The Leeds family, who owned CMP, walked away enormously wealthy.

Ken walked away disappointed.

Not long after, Computer Associates became a Diamond Sponsor of our CloudEXPO events and stayed one for years.

That's how business often worked in those days—relationships first, contracts later.

* * *

Another story Maureen broke involved Oracle co-president Charles Phillips.

His former mistress rented billboards in Times Square, Atlanta, and San Francisco, displaying photos of the two of them together and linking to a website documenting their eight-and-a-half-year affair.

The story exploded.

Phillips told Maureen that Larry Ellison had paid for the billboards.

She ran with it.

The article pulled in more than two hundred thousand reads over a single weekend.

* * *

At the time, Phillips was widely viewed as a potential successor to Ellison at Oracle.

Not long after the scandal, Oracle hired Mark Hurd as co-president, and Phillips stepped down.

He soon resurfaced as CEO of Infor, where he later became one of our Diamond Sponsors—paying double for the CloudEXPO opening keynote and taking the slot Oracle had held since the show's inception.

* * *

While all of this was unfolding, Maureen got into a public war with Pamela Jones—known online as PJ—the anonymous author of *Groklaw*.

Maureen attempted to unmask her identity publicly.

It was a disaster.

* * *

Groklaw's readers came after us in force.

Advertisers threatened to pull out.

Editors threatened to resign.

Our websites were hit with denial-of-service attacks.

We couldn't keep the servers online.

SYS-CON Media was suddenly collateral damage in a war I never asked to be part of.

The controversy spilled into mainstream media, including a *Forbes* cover story titled "Attack of the Blogs."

SYS-CON and the entire mess were now on display for the business world to analyze.

In the end, to protect the company, we pulled the article and stopped publishing Maureen's work.

I never asked her about her sources, and she never offered them.

But years later, I strongly suspected they were tied to Microsoft, which at the time was quietly backing SCO's legal campaign against Linux and IBM.

Whether that was true or not almost didn't matter.

What mattered was the lesson.

When you build platforms at scale, you don't just publish content—you inherit consequences.

Intent doesn't protect you. Distance doesn't protect you. Once you're big enough, everything sticks. That chapter taught me something I'd keep relearning: You don't get to choose which fires come with growth.

You only get to decide which ones you put out.

CHAPTER 17

We Hired a COO.
Thirty Days Later, He Was Gone.

Hiring and Firing a COO

Our newly hired COO arrived on the recommendation of Richard Mead — our investment banker at Jordan Edmiston Group. Think of Richard like the realtor who has your listing: he said, "Get a Chief Operating Officer."

We got one.

On his first day, I walked into Robert's office and told him to order a BlackBerry for our new COO.

Robert set it up, handed it over, and said with a grin, "All the management team has BlackBerries. This is yours. Keep it under your pillow at night."

* * *

The next morning, the COO stormed back to Robert, returning the device.

"I followed your instructions," he said, "but it kept ringing all night. I didn't get a wink of sleep."

Robert looked at him calmly and explained, "Fuat expects his management team to respond to emails within sixty seconds, 24/7. He doesn't sleep much and shares ideas with six managers around the clock. Welcome aboard — you're the seventh."

The COO shook his head, bewildered.

"I've never experienced anything like this in my career," he said, leaving the BlackBerry on Robert's desk. "I don't need it."

And so began our first industry recruit.

He arrived at 9 a.m., took a forty-five-minute lunch break, and left promptly at 5 p.m.

To this day, I have no idea what filled those eight hours on his factory–time-card schedule as our Chief Operating Officer. I never gave him a task, he never attended management meetings, and I doubt he ever fully understood what we did as a business.

When I finally let him go, his attorney called.

"My client will become a whistleblower unless you pay him," the lawyer said, demanding a sum that sounded larger than the COO's entire annual salary.

I told him to give his client my regards — and to blow his whistle in court so we could all hear what tune he had in mind.

We never heard from the COO or his lawyer again.

* * *

Later, I learned this wasn't his first rodeo.

Apparently, he had tried the exact same "whistleblower" stunt at his previous employer.

So why did my management team survive with me?

After I hired each of them, none of them quit.

Most joined SYS-CON Media straight out of college. Carmen recruited sales managers from Ramapo College, a small school just around the corner from our office, and Jim brought in the designers and editors.

I didn't touch the hiring process.

I was much better at firing people who didn't fit in.

During our first year, Jim came to me with a problem.

"We need a full-time web designer."

I said, "Go ahead, hire someone."

He put an ad in the *Rockland Journal News*: *Junior Web Designer Wanted*.

Resumes poured in, and Jim interviewed half a dozen candidates. Finally, he said he was ready to make an offer — but there was one small hitch.

"What is it?" I asked.

"I'm not sure if my favorite candidate is even at legal age to work," Jim said.

Turns out, the kid had spent the entire summer playing video games in his bedroom. His mother, seeing our ad, thought it was perfect for him and slipped the paper under his door.

That's how he ended up at the interview.

Jim hesitated.

"We can't ask his age — it's against the law. We can't ask if he's married, or where he's from, or anything like that."

So what did he do?

He called the high school principal.

"This kid came for a job interview," he explained, "but we're not sure if he's old enough to work legally."

The principal assured him he was sixteen.

Problem solved.

We hired him as a part-time intern — a student employee.

And just like that, our youngest web designer ever joined the team — half gamer, half code wizard — and helped shape SYS-CON Media's early years.

Two years later, Robert's high school graduation arrived.

By then, Louis had already started an office pool — one dollar per person — on whether we would ever hear from Robert again once he left for college.

Most bets predicted complete radio silence by September.

Just before driving up to his dorm at Syracuse, Robert stopped by my office.

He told me he planned to keep working from his dorm room and would send his hours to Joan.

I nodded politely, fully aware that Louis was already counting his winnings.

Four years passed.

Robert graduated from Syracuse University, diploma in hand, and Louis immediately launched Pool Number Two: would Robert come back full time now that he had a college degree and the entire world at his feet?

Once again, Robert ruined everyone's odds.

He showed up and returned to his job full time, proving that the safest bet in our office was always betting against the office pool.

My only hobby was my job. Back to the days of preparing our offering memorandum. I worked seven days a week and never quite understood why Saturdays and Sundays were on the calendar at all. What I did wasn't work — it was my most pleasurable occupation. A lucky hobby, really, with a payroll. I didn't do it because it was my company. I did it because I loved the job.

It never felt like work — just something I couldn't wait to get back to. I was exactly the same at my last known job at Rhône-Poulenc, the French chemical company in New Jersey. I worked seven days a week there, too, and was always puzzled by the empty building on weekends — and by the mass disappearance of people after 5 p.m. Monday through Friday.

* * *

One Saturday morning at Rhône-Poulenc, I ran into Bernie Kranz, our MIS director, at the coffee machine. Back then, IT was still called MIS — Management Information Systems. Bernie casually said, "When you get a chance, come by my office." At the time, my direct supervisor was Randy Hompesh. Randy reported to Jim Purcell. Jim reported to Bernie. Bernie reported to Tom Headly, vice president of finance. Tom ultimately reported to the president, John Wistrich.

* * *

I stepped into Bernie's corner office.

"Sit down," he said.

Then he looked at me seriously.

"Fuat, I see you here late every night. Most weekends too."

I asked, "Bernie, where's my department? Shouldn't they be here? We're rolling out our sales-force automation system for animal nutrition next week in Atlanta."

He continued.

"You don't belong here in the corporate world. You're an entrepreneur. You should be running your own business."

"Your coworkers — the people on the floor — their only goal is to retire with a good pension. Don't expect anyone to join you on a weekend. They aren't paid to care."

"They think like workers, not business owners."

"My advice? Find an idea. Start your own business. Stop waiting for others to work as hard as you do — they won't."

CHAPTER 18

We were among America's fastest-growing companies three years in a row.

Faster Than Anyone Expected

In Adam Sandler's Netflix movie *Murder Mystery*, there's a scene I always remember between Jennifer Aniston and the race car driver.

Jennifer leans in, clearly annoyed.

"You don't understand English, do you?"

He smiles and nods.

"Yes. Fast. Very fast."

Of course, the joke is that he understands—and speaks—perfect English.

That scene has always reminded me of SYS-CON.

* * *

Yes. We were fast. Very fast.

But we kept it low-key—almost like Lieutenant Columbo: unassuming, slightly disheveled, quietly sharp. People underestimated us, and we were perfectly fine with that.

Yes, Powersoft inserting our subscription cards into their product boxes was pure dumb luck. No argument there. But once that miracle happened, we weren't dumb—and we certainly didn't rely on luck every day after. We grabbed the ball, put our heads down, and ran straight for the finish line.

If I had to summarize the five years from 1994 to 1999 as briefly as possible, I'd say this:

I accidentally enrolled in a full-contact business startup crash course.

At the beginning of 1994, my home became the company address—and the company office.

It worked great.

Until it didn't.

Twelve months later, I was evicted from my own townhouse.

Why did the condo association throw me out of my own home?

First, AT&T knocked on my next-door neighbor's door and asked if they could use her attic. Naturally, she asked why. The technician casually explained they were there to install twelve new phone lines—for me.

That was disaster number one.

She immediately reported me to the condo association.

* * *

Then, twice in the same week, two different semi-trailer trucks tried—barely—to navigate our quiet little streets. Both rang the wrong doorbell looking for me.

Both were there to unload 10,000 books, stacked neatly on eight pallets.

And I almost forgot—before those books arrived, the printer in Brooklyn had already shipped 10,000 copies of our first issue to my condo.

That was our company address.

Where else would they ship them?

That turned disasters number two and three into one glorious, cata-strophic combo.

* * *

Only if we were located in an industrial complex with loading docks would we get that kind of cargo traffic.

UPS and FedEx deliveries were already nonstop, all day long. The trucks, the traffic, the doorbells—it never ended.

Soon after, I received a cease-and-desist letter from the association's attorney.

Not long after that came the court order.

I had to leave.

* * *

Urgently, we packed up and moved into a tiny office space in Pearl River that we rented from a pizza man.

It wasn't glamorous—but it worked.

And three years later, we occupied the entire ground floor of a Class-A office building at

135 Chestnut Ridge Road in Montvale.

Yes. Fast. Very fast.

* * *

How did we grow that fast—like the race car driver who drove Jennifer Aniston crazy?

First, I refused to commute between Pearl River and Jersey City.

I worked as long as I could during the day. Then, sometime after midnight, I crawled under the conference room table and passed out.

I woke up just before Nancy arrived for work around 7:00 a.m., brushed myself off, and pretended this was all part of a carefully designed productivity system.

It worked.

Exceptionally well.

Seven days a week.

* * *

In a nutshell, we made it onto the *Inc. 500* list—America's fastest-growing private companies—three years in a row.

It took a little luck, a lot of hard work, and an unhealthy amount of strategic planning.

Yes. Fast. Very fast.

* * *

In 1999, *Milliyet*, a Turkish newspaper, profiled SYS-CON's inclusion among America's fastest-growing companies.

THE FASTEST GROWING TURK IN THE U.S.

In 1999, a Turkish-born entrepreneur named Fuat Kircaali was listed among America's 500 fastest-growing business leaders. The company behind the recognition, SYS-CON, began not with venture capital or a business plan, but with a $1,500 cash advance taken from a credit card.

From a modest office near a New York taxi stand, SYS-CON grew into a multi-million-dollar publishing and media company serving the global technology industry. Founded in 1994, the company reached a valuation of $30 million in five years and began preparing for a public offering.

SYS-CON became known for its influential developer publications, including Java Developers Journal, PowerBuilder Developer's Journal, ColdFusion Developer's Journal, Object Magazine, Delphi Journal, and Tango Journal—titles read by hundreds of thousands of software professionals worldwide.

At a time when technology publishing lacked depth and specialization, SYS-CON filled a critical gap by focusing directly on developers.

* * *

Kircaali was born in Eskişehir, Turkey, and studied computer science at Boğaziçi University before continuing graduate work at the University of Zurich in Switzerland. He arrived in the United States as an intern in 1984 and spent the next decade gaining hands-on experience in technology companies before launching SYS-CON.

The company's culture mirrored its founder's unconventional path. SYS-CON rejected rigid corporate norms in favor of flexible hours, casual dress, and a strong emphasis on trust. Many employees joined while still in school and grew into senior editorial and leadership roles.

By the late 1990s, SYS-CON was posting double-digit annual growth and receiving regular acquisition offers. Kircaali declined them, choosing independence and long-term vision over early exits.

"Our goal was never growth at any cost," Kircaali said at the time.

"It was growth without losing our humanity."

What began as a risk funded on a credit card became a defining chapter in American tech publishing—and a case study in how instinct, timing, and trust can outperform conventional business wisdom.

Carmen and I spent Thanksgiving in Hudson County Prison.

Thanksgiving In Prison

B ack in 1995, long before any of that, we were living in pure survival mode—working nearly twenty hours a day on almost no sleep.

At five in the morning, I'd load post office bins into my beat-up Honda Civic, drop mail at the Manhattan post office, drive through the Holland Tunnel, and head straight to work.

Eventually, that pace caught up with us.

* * *

Here's how we ended up spending the night in jail—at least as I remember it.

* * *

Carmen and I got into an argument. About what, I honestly don't remember. Emotions escalated, and at some point she called 911. Things moved fast. I heard sirens, looked out the bay window, and saw multiple police cars with lights flashing. Neighbors gathered in the street. The officers came inside and focused on Carmen. One of them recognized me from years earlier, and we acknowledged each other.

A senior officer asked Carmen why she had called.

She said she felt threatened and wanted to press charges.

The officers spoke with both of us. From my perspective, they seemed skeptical and asked several follow-up questions.

Eventually, they explained that if charges were pursued, arrests would have to be made so things could be sorted out at the precinct.

Carmen said she wanted to proceed.

* * *

She was handcuffed and taken outside.

A short time later, I was handcuffed as well.

With neighbors watching.

It was humiliating.

That night was one of the lowest and most surreal moments of my life.

* * *

We were taken to the Jersey City central precinct, fingerprinted, photographed, then transported to the county jail.

We were each allowed one phone call and told someone could pick us up by posting a $50 bail.

* * *

Carmen didn't call her parents on Thanksgiving Eve.

She called a friend.

No answer.

I called Engin.

No answer either.

He later told me he'd been at a biker bar in Pearl River with Claudia and never heard the phone ring.

With no one reachable, we were processed, handed orange jail uniforms, and placed in general population.

About twenty-four hours later, on Monday morning, the judge dismissed the charges.

We were released outside the Hudson County courthouse still wearing our orange uniforms, with HUDSON COUNTY PRISON printed across the back.

It was freezing.

* * *

I tried flagging down a police car.

"We were just released," I said. "We have no cash. Can you give us a ride home?"

The officer rolled his eyes and drove off.

Eventually, we made our way home, left our temporary prison ID cards on the kitchen table, changed into regular clothes, then drove back to the jail to retrieve our belongings.

* * *

While we were gone, Marilyn—my ex-wife—stopped by the house.

She took the prisoner ID cards, complete with our high-resolution mug shots, glued them back-to-back, sealed them in acrylic, and turned them into a keychain.

She proudly showed it to her coworkers.

CHAPTER 20

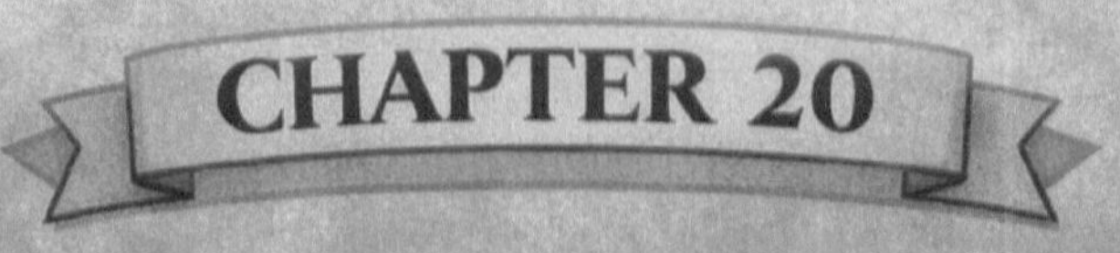

God Doesn't Think He's Larry Ellison.

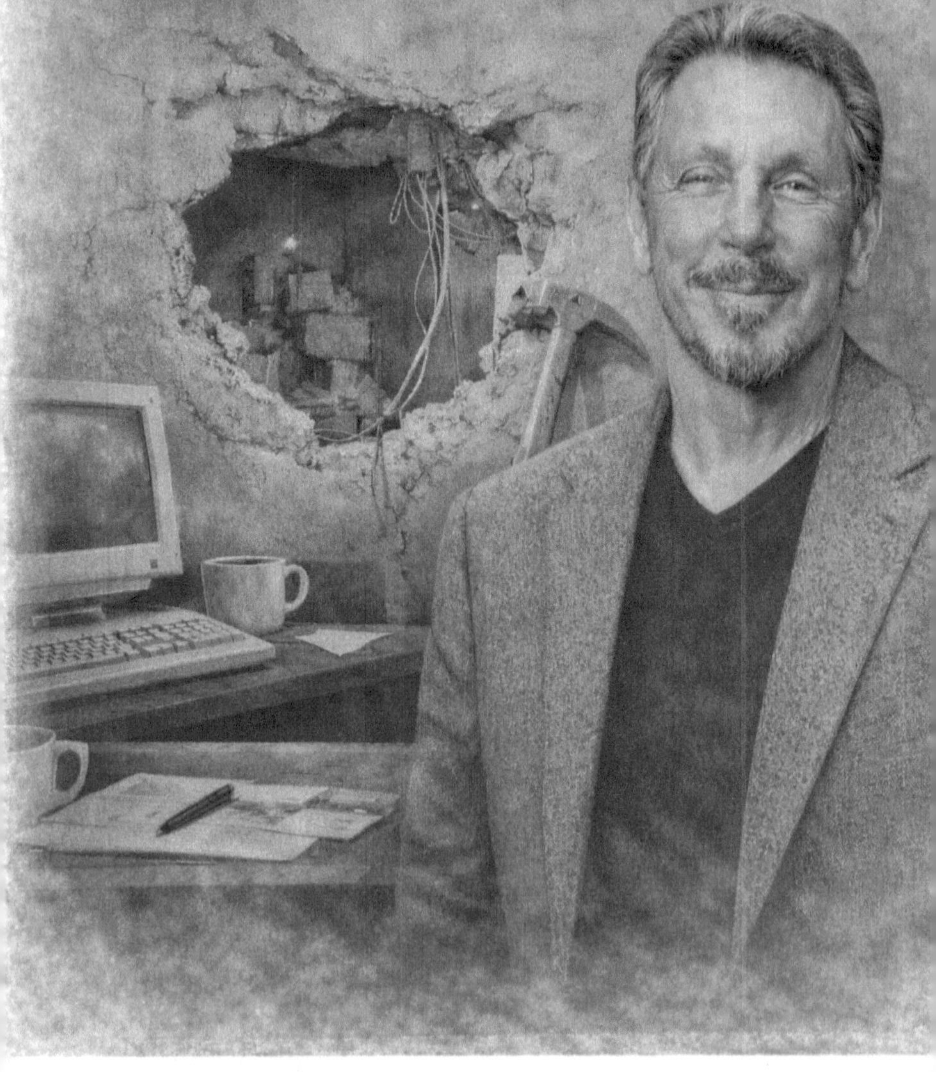

God Doesn't Think He's Larry Ellison

In 1997, I was technically homeless.

I worked eighteen hours a day and slept in the conference room at 39 East Central Avenue—our Pearl River office. The lights never really went off. Neither did my mind.

* * *

Around that time, a new Larry Ellison book had just been released. I picked up a copy at Barnes & Noble. It turned out to be far more compelling than I expected.

In *The Difference Between God and Larry Ellison: God Doesn't Think He's Larry Ellison*, author Mike Wilson explored Ellison's early years and the mindset that shaped Oracle. One story in particular stayed with me. It came from Bruce Scott, one of Oracle's earliest employees and a key technical figure in the company's beginnings.

Scott described his first experience working with Ellison at SDL, before the company was even called Oracle. He was trying to connect computer terminals between two rooms when he ran into a wall. When he asked Ellison how they were supposed to route the wiring through, Ellison didn't hesitate. He picked up a hammer and smashed a hole straight through it.

Scott later said that moment captured Ellison's entire philosophy.

Find a way—or make one.

In the 1990s, media still ruled the technology world. Before the internet, the only way software companies could announce new products was through press tours to magazines. Executives flew in constantly, scheduling back-to-back meetings with publishers like us.

Our office sat above Yossi's Bagels. The roof leaked. The walls were cracked. There were holes we kept meaning to fix and never did. Yet despite the surroundings, we had become one of the top technology publishers in the country.

PR teams grew accustomed to the contrast—polished executives in expensive suits walking into a visibly worn office. We, in turn, grew used to the expressions on their faces.

* * *

That night, after finishing Bruce Scott's story, I slipped a piece of paper into the book to mark the page and fell asleep under the conference room table.

The next morning, we had PR visitors scheduled.

Three or four people walked in. Gail Schultz greeted them, and business cards were passed around the table.

As introductions went around, I heard one man say his name.

"Bruce Scott."

I leaned forward, reached for the book, opened it to the page I had marked the night before, and looked up.

"This Bruce Scott?" I asked.

He laughed.

"Yes," he said.

That morning, sitting in a leaking office above a bagel shop, we talked about Oracle's earliest days—the same story I had read just hours earlier, now suddenly seated across the table from me.

* * *

I had read his story the night before, alone in the dark.

By morning, it was sitting across the table from me.

In my world, that's how things always seemed to happen.

CHAPTER 21

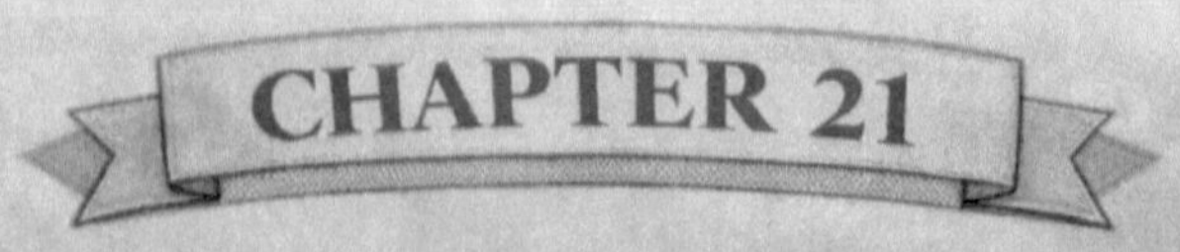

I met with Jim Fawcette, and the bank asked me to run my biggest competitor.

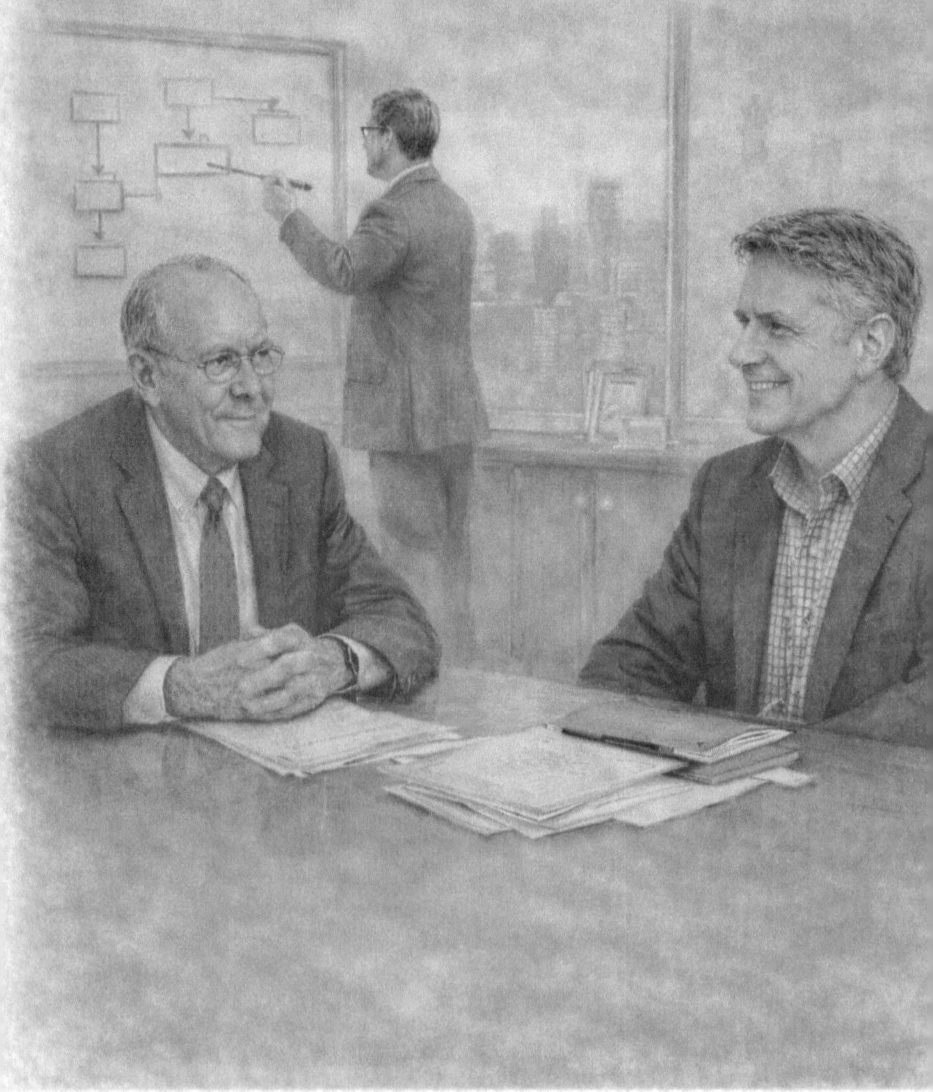

The Merger That Never Happened

In early 2007, one of the most respected names in developer publishing quietly came to an end.

Fawcette Technical Publications — founded and led by Jim Fawcette, and best known for *Visual Studio Magazine* and industry conferences like VS Live! — was acquired by 1105 Media and folded into its Redmond Media Group.

What had once operated as an independent, founder-driven media company became part of a larger corporate publishing machine.

It marked the close of an era in technical media — and the beginning of a very different chapter for those of us who had lived through that world firsthand.

Jim Fawcette was my absolute publishing idol.

Whenever I stopped at Barnes & Noble, I would flip through the pages of *Visual Studio Magazine*, study his photo on the "From the Publisher" page, and feel completely intimidated.

For the very first issue of *PowerBuilder Developer's Journal*, I even went to Sears Photo Studio and took a picture deliberately imitating his.

I wanted to be Jim Fawcette when I grew up.

It never once occurred to me that one day I would put him out of business — right after Rick Friedman.

Jim Fawcette launched *JavaPro*.

Rick Friedman launched *Java Report*.

Both came after *Java Developer's Journal*.

And somehow, without intending to — and certainly without celebrating it — I outlasted them both.

Not because I was smarter.

Not because I had more money.

But because timing, speed, and relentless execution mattered more than reputation.

The people I once studied from newsstand racks — the publishers I admired most — became my competitors.

And then, quietly, they were gone.

I used to get phone calls from strangers in my office.

This was another one of those calls.

"Fuat?" the man said. "I'm calling from Washington, D.C. We're a bank that specializes in financing publishing and media companies. Fawcette Technical Publications is one of our portfolio companies. I'd like to set up a meeting with you at our office."

A few days later, I drove to Washington. It was about three hours.

I met the banker who had called me. He explained that the bank had extended multiple loans to Fawcette Technical Publications — and that, effectively, they now controlled the company.

Then he laid out his idea.

He wanted me to merge SYS-CON Media with Fawcette Technical Publications and run the combined entity.

It was, in essence, a merger proposal.

We didn't discuss structure or valuation in detail. He said that if I was interested in principle, he would bring Jim into the conversation and we'd explore whether a win-win deal could be created.

I said sure. Let's talk.

At the next meeting, I found myself sitting in the same conference room with the banker — and with Jim Fawcette.

The man I once tried to imitate.

The banker stood at the whiteboard, drawing boxes and arrows. One company flowed into another. Lines connected debt to assets. Arrows pointed forward.

As he spoke, something became very clear.

Jim was deeply in debt to the bank.

I sat there stunned.

How could that even be possible?

I was sitting on roughly $18 million in cash, listening to the banker explain how the company I once idolized had been slowly buried under leverage.

By the time he finished, the conclusion was obvious.

A merger would not help SYS-CON Media in any way.

We had even turned down acquiring *Streaming Media* from Tom Kemp — a company he had paid $100 million for and later offered to me for $200,000.

We weren't chasing trophies.

We were happy growing at our own speed — profitably, carefully, and in control.

So I declined.

The meeting ended politely.

That was the last time I ever saw Jim Fawcette.

Years earlier, I had stood in Barnes & Noble holding his magazine, studying his photo, wondering if I'd ever belong in the same industry.

Now I was driving home from Washington, having just been asked to run his company — and choosing not to.

There was no victory lap.

No celebration.

Just a quiet realization.

In business, admiration doesn't protect you.

Reputation doesn't save you.

And being first doesn't guarantee you'll still be standing at the end.

Only execution does.

And sometimes, the strangest moment of success isn't when you beat your heroes—

It's when you realize they're gone,

and you're still here.

ACT II — THE PEAK

Momentum is a dangerous thing.

Once it starts, it convinces you that it will never end.

Ideas turned into magazines. Magazines turned into conferences. Conferences turned into an industry. Money arrived faster than experience, and success created the illusion of control.

This was the era of speed — of growth without brakes and confidence without caution. The phones never stopped ringing. The calendar never cleared. And every "yes" carried a cost I wouldn't understand until much later.

At the top, everything looks permanent.

It never is.

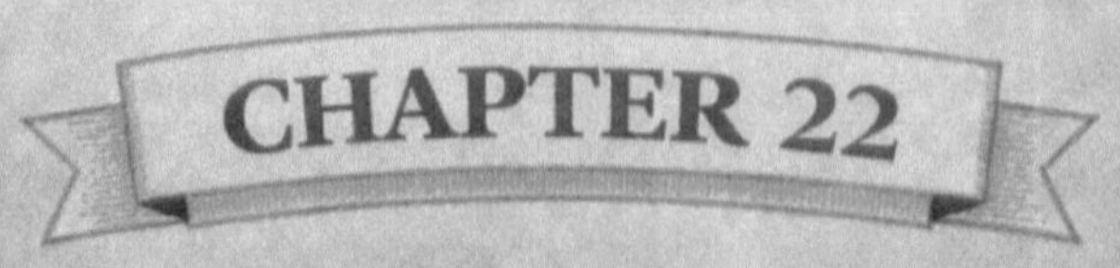

CHAPTER 22

Tom Kemp, David Nussbaum,
and Wilma Jordan—
and the $50 million phone call.

The $50 Million Call

In September 2000, I was sitting in my office when the phone rang. I didn't recognize the number.

The voice on the other end belonged to a stranger.

"Hello, Fuat. My name is Tom Kemp," he said. "I'm the CEO of Penton Media. We're based in Cleveland, Ohio. We believe Penton and SYS-CON Media have strong synergies."

There it was—synergies. The word always arrives early.

He continued without pause. "The president of Penton Media, David Nussbaum, and I would like to meet you for dinner."

Before hanging up, he added, "Please write down this phone number for Wilma Jordan. Tell her I gave it to you."

I called Wilma immediately.

After I explained who I was and how I had gotten her number, she burst out laughing.

"Tom Kemp just bought Duke Communications from David Duke for fifty million dollars in cash," she said. "We represented David."

Then she kept going.

"Our company, the Jordan Edmiston Group, will serve as your investment banker. We will represent you in the sale of SYS-CON Media. As a full-service firm, we not only prepare your offering memorandum, reach out to prospective buyers, and negotiate for the highest possible price, but we also provide psychological support services to our clients."

She paused, then added a story.

"David Duke lost his composure after receiving fifty million dollars in cash from Tom Kemp. He traveled to China in an attempt to rid the world of nuclear weapons. Everyone lost contact with him after he refused to meet with our psychologist."

Then she laughed again.

Duke Communications was a publishing and media company based in Loveland, Colorado, known for its trade and technology properties. It published titles such as Windows 2000 Magazine, SQL Server Magazine, NEWS/400, and Business Finance, and operated related digital media, email newsletters, websites, and training networks.

Penton Media, by contrast, was a major U.S. business-to-business media company with roots dating back to the early 1900s. It published trade magazines, directories, and electronic information products, produced industry events and conferences, and expanded into digital media services over time. In the late 1990s and early 2000s, under Tom Kemp, Penton pursued an aggressive growth-by-acquisition strategy, buying numerous niche media and events businesses.

In 2000, Penton Media acquired Duke Communications in a strategic move designed to integrate Duke's strong technology media brands and audience into Penton's portfolio. The equity purchase agreement was signed on August 29, 2000, between Penton and Duke's principal owner, David A. Duke, along with associated family trusts. The structure included an initial cash payment, with contemporary reports estimating the total potential value at up to $150 million—approximately $100 million at closing and up to $50 million in contingent earn-outs tied to future performance. The acquisition closed in September 2000.

Just over a year later, the post-9/11 economic downturn hit. Advertising-dependent media and technology sectors were devastated. Performance metrics across the industry collapsed. The contingent earn-outs were never realized, and David Duke walked away from the deal with only fifty million dollars in his pocket.

The word on the street was that Tom Kemp liked round numbers. In his most recent acquisitions, he had paid exactly fifty million dollars each time.

Shortly after our phone call, I drove to New York City and met with Wilma's team. Richard Mead was assigned to handle our account. We sat down together and reviewed the entire process in detail.

Preparing the offering memorandum would take about six months. For each magazine title we published, we maintained a separate profit-and-loss statement dating back to its launch, with cost accounting detailed down to the individual page.

At the time, we were publishing twelve titles, all distributed on major newsstands worldwide and carried in every Borders and Barnes & Noble store across the United States.

These individual product P&Ls were rolled up into the overall company P&L and balance sheet.

Wilma's accountants soon moved into our office. We gave them our main conference room and the keys so they could work undisturbed. They began a thorough audit of our financial records. Several times a day, auditors came into my office with questions only I could answer.

One day, one of them sat down and said, "We've noticed that you drive a bulletproof Mercedes S600, Carmen drives an SL500, and Jim Morgan drives a Lexus SUV. But we can't figure out who's driving the brand-new white Nissan Altima—a fully customized one with custom leather seats."

I told him we didn't have an Altima.

He pointed to the paperwork. "It's right here on the books. The company is making monthly payments for it."

I went to Joan, who ran the books. She knew nothing about the Altima. She walked over to the next cubicle to ask Judith, but Judith wasn't at her desk.

After a few days of investigation, we discovered the truth. Judith, from accounts payable, had leased the car in the company's name for her own personal use.

We never saw her again.

Through his auditors, Tom Kemp closely monitored the progress of our offering memorandum, and he liked what he saw.

Soon afterward, he called again. We arranged a dinner—just the three of us: Tom Kemp, David Nussbaum, and me—at Tavern on the Green in New York City.

When the waiter came to take our order, he delivered the same joke he'd used before. "Are you gentlemen still friends, or should I bring the steak knives?"

We all laughed.

During dinner, Tom explained that Wilma would share our offering memorandum—often referred to as the "black book," because the bound copies were presented in black vinyl covers—with a select group of prospective buyers.

"That's perfectly fine," he said. "That's just how the process works. In the end, we'll submit the strongest offer to acquire your company."

By then, the year was drawing to a close. Carmen and I were invited to Wilma's holiday reception at her Park Avenue apartment.

The elevator opened directly into her spacious living room.

Among the guests were the Austrian ambassador and his wife.

Another couple stood nearby, the husband excitedly describing how he had just purchased two thousand acres in Montana, making him neighbors with Ted Turner.

The preparation of the black book—and the entire process—took considerably longer than we had initially estimated.

* * *

Richard Mead suggested we needed to strengthen our management team for buyer presentations. He recommended hiring someone with a strong accounting background. I met with the candidate at our Montvale, New Jersey, office and brought him on board as Chief Operating Officer.

We promptly added his name to the management bios. Grisha Davida was already listed as president of SYS-CON Events.

During the interview, the new COO asked about fringe benefits. I asked what he currently had. He told me he was driving a company car—a Mercedes GLC 300.

I pointed out my own car through the window: a 1985 Honda Civic with 180,000 miles, every corner battered and damaged. He smiled and reminded me that I might need a new car myself.

Mid-interview, I left him in my office, stopped by Joan's desk, and said, "Please tell him we appreciate the meeting. We'll get back to him with an offer."

I then drove to Prestige Motors on Route 17 in Paramus. I walked in and told the salesman I wanted a black car with a big number in the back. He looked me up and down—cotton sticking out of my jacket collar from my beard, dirty jeans, worn shoes—and assumed I was homeless.

"You can buy any black car in the showroom and glue a big number on it," he said.

None of the salesmen took me seriously.

I went upstairs and found a man sitting in front of a computer. "Excuse me," I said. "Can you sell me a car? The salesmen downstairs seem busy."

"What kind of car?" he asked.

"I'd like a black car with a big number in the back."

"How about an S500?"

"I saw an S600 on the road. Do you have those?"

He checked the computer. "There's one coming in next week—a black S600—but it's bulletproof."

"Fine," I said. "Just charge me a fair price."

I gave him Joan's phone number. "Please wash it, prepare it, and bring it to my office. Joan will handle the paperwork and payment."

His name was Doug Tucker. We became friends. Over the years, I bought or leased about a dozen cars from him. He even gave me a nickname—CT.

"What's CT?" I asked.

He smiled. "Crazy Turk."

Eventually, the NDAs were signed, and the black books were shipped to approximately two dozen interested companies, including several based in London.

In the process of "strengthening the management team," I accidentally hired two executives—Cathy Walters and Grisha Davida—to run SYS-CON Events.

When both showed up on Monday morning ready to start work, I had a brief oops moment. Instead of letting either go, I kept them both. We reshuffled offices and split responsibilities. Cathy led conference content. Grisha oversaw sales. In today's dollars, each earned $376,448 a year.

I never believed in traditional management teams. Until then, I hadn't hired anyone from the industry. The seventy-two people on our payroll were all local hires. They grew up inside our culture, unburdened by the habits and borrowed thinking people bring from previous jobs.

The idea of strengthening the management team wasn't mine. It was the investment banker's.

Once word spread that SYS-CON Media was for sale, the process became educational. Our balance sheet showed sixteen million dollars in cash, which seemed to short-circuit most prospective buyers. They couldn't reconcile buying a company that actually had money.

One bidder submitted what could only be described as a joke offer: eighteen million dollars, with a note explaining they would "keep the cash."

Generous.

Our accountant fixed the problem quickly. Going forward, Carmen and I received two hundred thousand dollars each in monthly bonuses. The excess-cash issue vanished overnight.

While Wilma and Richard Mead were lining up boardroom presentations, we received a call from Advanstar Communications. Advanstar was a major U.S. B2B media and events company with a long history in trade shows, publications, and digital products, later absorbed into UBM's global events portfolio. Its longtime leader was Bob Krakoff.

Bob Krakoff wanted to meet.

Grisha and Cathy knew him well. I didn't know Bob Krakoff. I didn't know Advanstar. And until that moment, I didn't know they knew me.

Grisha and I left our Montvale office. We occupied the entire ground floor of an A-class building at 135 Chestnut Ridge Road, owned by Mack-Cali. I designed the space myself.

We furnished it with Steelcase ergonomic chairs that cost $1,200 each—about $2,258 in early-2026 dollars. They were the most expensive chairs I could find. I figured that if we were going to spend our lives sitting down, we might as well do it seriously.

As we walked out, Cathy Walters said, "Hey, say hi to Uncle Bob from me."

I asked how she knew him.

"I ran many trade shows for him," she said. "I always called him Uncle Bob."

We arrived at Advanstar's offices at 641 Lexington Avenue, on the eighth floor. Kerry Gumas, the company's president reporting to Bob Krakoff, greeted us and walked us to Bob's corner office.

Bob was in a hurry. The meeting lasted about thirty seconds.

"I hear Tom Kemp wants to buy you," he said. "I don't need your black book or your offering memorandum. Just write down your numbers and fax them to my plane. I'm on my way to California. I'll look them over and fax you back my offer."

Wilma Jordan advised me against it. She reminded me that she was representing SYS-CON Media and managing the entire process.

And that was that.

Bob Krakoff led Advanstar through a period of significant growth in print media, trade shows, and conferences from the late 1990s into the early 2000s. Under his leadership, the company published dozens of industry magazines and operated professional conferences and expositions worldwide. Recognizing that Advanstar's portfolio was weak in technology titles, Krakoff made those a priority in his acquisition strategy.

After retiring from Advanstar in 2004, he founded Blantyre Partners and collaborated with The Blackstone Group on business-to-business media investments. He later became president and CEO of Nielsen Business Media.

Bob Krakoff passed away in 2007 at his home in Boston at the age of seventy-one. At the time of his death, he was serving as president and CEO of Nielsen Business Media, which included publications such as Billboard, The Hollywood Reporter, and Adweek.

He had been brought out of his second retirement to join Nielsen following the nine-billion-dollar private-equity buyout of VNU Inc. The company was renamed Nielsen Co. the following January. Working closely with Chairman and CEO David Calhoun, Krakoff helped reshape Nielsen into the world's leading provider of authoritative data and marketing information. Those who worked with him recall that even in his brief tenure, he made substantial and lasting progress.

CHAPTER 23

Bob Krakow said,
"Send your one-page financials to my jet,
and I'll fax back a cash offer
before I land in San Francisco."

Closing Day: Fifty Million Dollars

That week, we were waiting to hear from Penton Media on the final acquisition terms for my company.

I kept asking Robert to check the fax machine three times a day.

Based on what Wilma had told me, we were expecting an offer of around $50 million. The formal proposal was scheduled to arrive on Friday, September 14, 2001.

* * *

On Monday, we were buried in deadlines and follow-ups — business as usual.

On Tuesday morning, Carmen stopped by my office on her way to the kitchen.

"A plane just hit the World Trade Center," she said. "Robin is worried. Her brother works in one of the buildings."

Within hours, we were watching history unfold in real time, along with the rest of the world.

* * *

As the magnitude of what had happened became clear, I said, "Everyone, please turn off the lights and go home."

I took a few of the younger staff with me, and we headed home together.

For the next twenty-four hours, we sat glued to the television — stunned, silent, trying to understand how everything had changed in a single morning.

* * *

We returned to work on Wednesday.

The next day, my phone rang. It was Tom Kemp.

"Fuat, everything has changed," he said. "The Javits Center is now being used as a triage center for the World Trade Center."

He continued, "I had InternetWorld scheduled there next week. There's no show."

I said, "Tom, my Web Services Edge conference was at the Javits the week after InternetWorld."

There was a long pause.

Then he said, "Fuat, I'm calling to let you know we've taken a massive hit. I'm not even sure we'll still be in business after the dust settles. There will be no acquisition of your company. It's over."

* * *

Then he added, almost apologetically, "But I feel terrible. I can sell you the Streaming Media show — practically give it to you — for $200,000. Send me a check and it's yours."

Just one year earlier, Penton had acquired Streaming Media, Inc. in a deal valued at up to $100 million — roughly $65 million paid up front, with an additional earn-out of up to $35 million tied to performance.

Now Tom was offering me an event he had effectively paid $65 million for — for $200,000.

I was furious.

I walked into Grisha's office and said, "Grisha, what is this? A bait and switch? What the hell am I supposed to do with Streaming Media? This is the biggest emotional whiplash of my life."

That was the last time I ever heard from Tom Kemp.

As he had predicted, Penton slowly melted away.

CHAPTER 24

We subpoenaed Dan Rather, Tom Krakow, and Peter Jennings.

The $7 Million AIG Refused To Pay

At the center of our legal battle was a single, almost unbelievable claim.

AIG argued that September 11 did not qualify as a terrorist event under the language of its insurance policies.

That position triggered a courtroom fight that would last three years.

* * *

As part of the discovery process, we subpoenaed the evening news anchors who had delivered the events of that day to the nation — Dan Rather, Tom Brokaw, and Peter Jennings.

When Hank Greenberg's lawyers received the subpoenas, my attorney, Alan Asher, got an immediate phone call.

"Let's settle the case."

While the litigation dragged on, Hank Greenberg appeared repeatedly on CNBC with Maria Bartiromo, publicly stating that AIG had already settled all 9/11-related claims.

That wasn't true.

For three years, our case remained unresolved while those statements continued to be made — misleading investors and the public alike.

The truth would eventually surface.

But not without a fight.

* * *

Before our case with AIG was finally settled, Greenberg was already gone.

In 2005, he was forced out as CEO of AIG following intense regulatory pressure stemming from accounting and disclosure investigations led by New York Attorney General Eliot Spitzer and federal regulators. The probes focused on alleged accounting practices that inflated AIG's earnings and misled investors. Although Greenberg denied wrongdoing and was never criminally charged, AIG's board pushed him to resign in an effort to stabilize the company and demonstrate cooperation with regulators.

His departure ended nearly four decades of control over AIG and marked the beginning of a massive restructuring period for the firm.

* * *

During those three years, my frustration boiled over more than once.

I remember telling my attorney, Alan Asher, that I wanted to put Hank Greenberg's face on every one of my magazine covers — twelve titles lined up on the Barnes & Noble newsstand — with a single headline underneath:

Crook.

Alan begged me not to do it.

He was right.

Some battles are won in court.

Others are won by waiting.

Three years later, we settled our millions of dollars in show-cancellation losses with AIG.

They had only one condition, which I accepted: the settlement amount would remain confidential.

To this day, only my attorney, my accountant, and I know the exact amount of the check I received from Hank Greenberg.

CHAPTER 25

I wanted to hire KC and the
Sunshine Band
and hear KC sing
"Boogie Shoes."

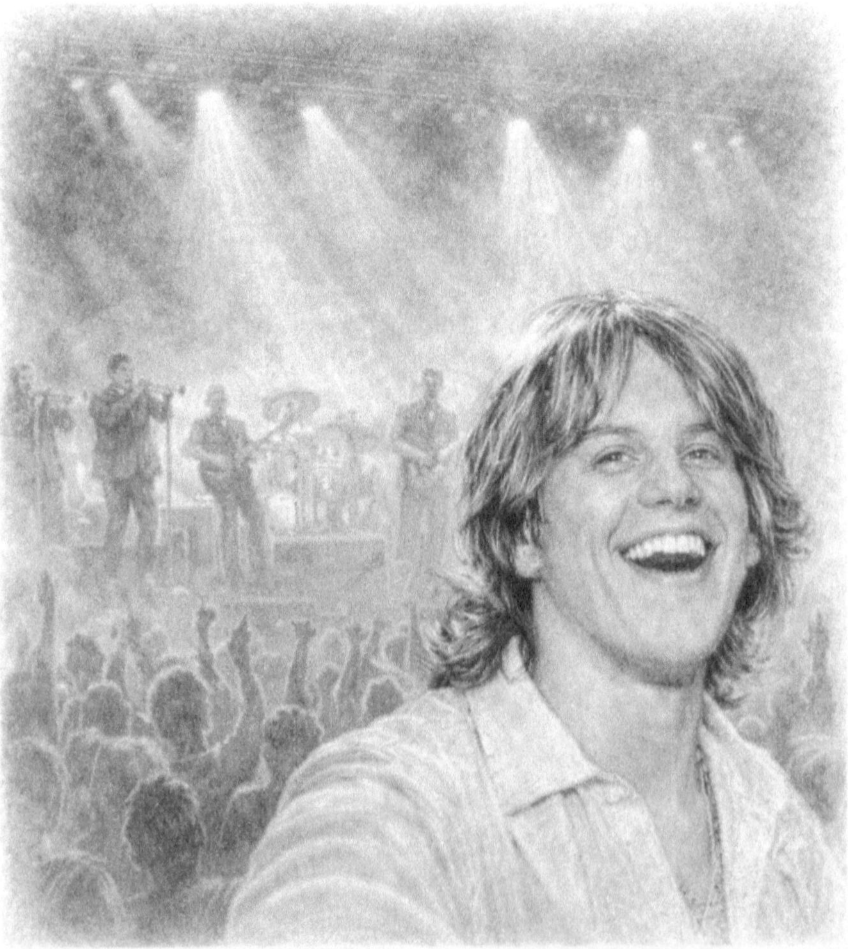

The Night I Booked The Temptations

Corinna called me from my office.

She said Carmen and the team had just wrapped a planning meeting for our upcoming CloudEXPO Silicon Valley at the Santa Clara Convention Center. Someone had floated a bold idea: a private concert during the opening reception. A real band. A name people would recognize. She wanted my opinion.

I said,

"Can we get KC and the Sunshine Band? I want to hear KC sing *Boogie Shoes* live."

That fantasy lasted about five minutes. They were on tour in Canada and completely unavailable.

The booking people suggested a few other options that could work with our California dates.

Corinna called back.

"Out of everyone who's available," she said, "we picked The Temptations."

I paused for half a second, then said,

"Yesss. I love *My Girl*. Are they still around? They must be a hundred years old."

Next, we rented a few billboards around Silicon Valley to promote the event. One of the rotating banners Louis designed featured The Temptations. When the billboards went live, someone sent me a couple of photos. There it was—our conference logo, our dates, and The Temptations—towering over traffic like a very soulful tech announcement.

Around that same time, my mornings followed a very different rhythm.

When I was at my Florida deepwater mansion, I spent a lot of time at a Starbucks on Federal Highway in Deerfield Beach. I always sat outside, usually near the trash container, smoking cigarettes and drinking coffee. The seating arrangement wasn't exactly curated. Our table was surrounded by a regular cast of homeless folks, and after a few days, everyone knew everyone. Same faces. Same seats. Same routines.

I'm pretty sure our table had a reputation.

Not "the tech CEO table."

Not "the conference organizer table."

It was the homeless table.

Most of the people there actually were homeless. I just happened to be the guy running a major tech conference, launching a billboard campaign, and booking a legendary Motown group—while sitting next to a garbage can, chain-smoking, and blending right in. If anything, I probably looked more homeless than they did.

Then I tweeted one of the billboard photos.

My phone buzzed immediately.

The text read:

"Fuat, those five guys on your billboard are NOT The Temptations. They're just five random Black guys. You're going to get sued for calling them The Temptations."

Apparently, Louis had used a random stock photo.

At Starbucks, two women were having lunch at the next table. I'd seen them there for months. They had that unmistakable lawyer energy—confident voices, precise language, the kind of tone that sounds billable. I leaned over.

"You guys sound like lawyers," I said. "I have a question."

They looked up.

"I just hired The Temptations," I continued. "We put up billboards announcing a private concert, but our designer used the wrong photo. Not actually them. Are we going to get sued for this?"

Both women stared at me.

And I knew exactly what they were thinking.

Perfect. One of the local homeless guys has officially lost it—now he thinks he hired The Temptations.

CHAPTER 26

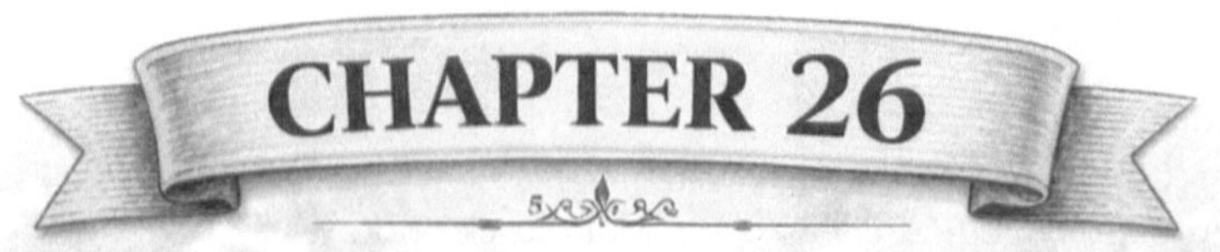

At the last rest stop before leaving New Jersey, the idea hit me—fully formed.

Cloud computing.

"Put me on speaker," I told Carmen.

After I finished, Jeremy asked,

"What *the fuck is cloud computing?"*

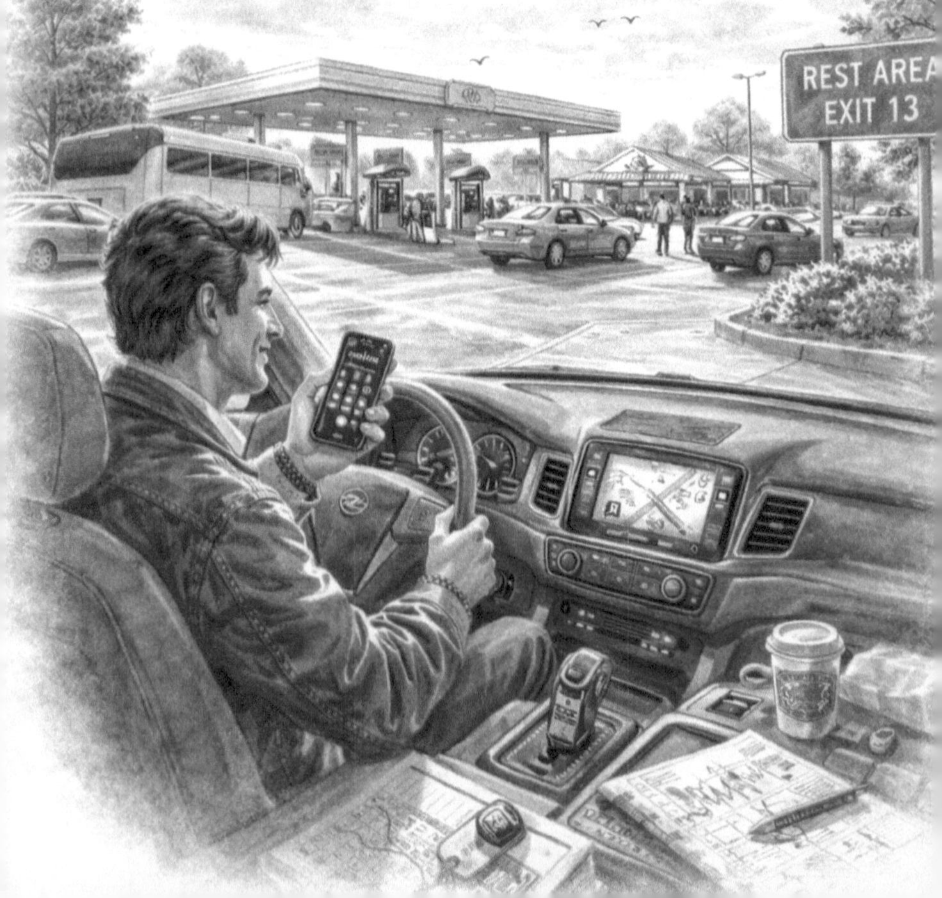

Coined "Cloud Computing"

I like to drive between New Jersey and Florida. About 1,200 miles, door to door.

I enjoy it.

The road clears my head. Somewhere around Virginia, the noise drops out and the meetings begin — not on Zoom, not on the phone, but in my head. I replay conversations, argue both sides, and solve problems that wouldn't budge at a desk. By the time I arrive, the decisions are already made.

I once read that Luciano Pavarotti loved driving long distances too. He could have flown anywhere instantly, but often chose the road instead. Flying took control away from him. Driving gave it back.

The car became a moving buffer between life and performance, chaos and focus. He arrived calmer, centered, ready.

That made sense to me.

Driving isn't wasted time. It's transitional time.

Airports compress everything — arrival, pressure, expectations — into a single moment. The road stretches it out. Mile by mile, the mind organizes itself. Thoughts line up. Noise settles. You don't arrive abruptly; you arrive prepared.

For Pavarotti, the road protected his voice.

For me, it protects my thinking.

Different instruments. Same discipline.

Some people measure travel by speed. Others measure it by what gets resolved along the way.

I've always preferred the second kind.

I made many business decisions — and launched more than a few products — while driving long distances alone.

This is one of them.

* * *

On a Saturday morning, I walked into the office. Carmen, Robert, Alex, and Jeremy were already there.

"Guys, I'm driving to Florida," I said. "I'll see you soon. I've got my BlackBerry. I'm online. No worries."

Then I walked out, got in the car, and pointed it toward the New Jersey Turnpike.

At the last rest stop before leaving New Jersey, the idea hit me — fully formed.

Cloud computing.

I pulled out my phone and called the office in Montvale.

"Put me on speaker," I told Carmen.

The entire management team gathered around the conference table while I stood alone in a highway rest area, staring at traffic and coffee machines.

I didn't explain the idea.

I didn't pitch it.

I gave instructions.

"Robert — secure the website URLs."

"Alex — start branding. Logos. Visual identity."

"Jeremy — build the content. Put meat on the website."

"Carmen — call the Javits Center. Wake up the sales team and lock in June dates."

There was a pause.

Then I said, "Ladies and gentlemen — on Monday morning at 7:00 a.m., we are launching CloudEXPO."

Silence.

Finally, Jeremy broke it.

"What the fuck is cloud computing?"

Carmen cut him off immediately.

"Just do what he's asking," she said. "You know how this works. Whenever he comes up with one of these ideas, it turns into something big."

She paused, then laughed.

"Remember when he announced Java Developer's Journal? Other publishers were laughing at us. They said we were making a magazine for Starbucks."

Then she added, "Whatever the fuck cloud computing is — let's just do it." They had laughed at us before. By the time a few competitors finally figured out Java — after we had already published twelve issues — we had put two of them out of business.

I could smell the cloud from a mile away.

* * *

That week in Silicon Valley, we sold out the entire expo floor. Carmen even added tabletop exhibit space on the bridge connecting the convention center to the hotel. She squeezed ten exhibitors onto that overpass.

After the David Linthicum keynote, we opened the expo floor.

David spoke about web services — and during his talk, he sensed something brewing.

When attendees poured out afterward, they didn't head toward the main hall.

They rushed the hotel bridge.

I turned to Carmen.

"What are those tabletop exhibits selling?"

Before she could answer, the fire marshal showed up. The walkway to the hotel was completely blocked.

She shrugged.

"They're all talking about something... cloud."

* * *

That Saturday, during my 1,200-mile drive back to Florida, I replayed the entire California event in my head. The keynote. The bottleneck. The bridge. The word everyone kept repeating. That's when it hit me.

* * *

That realization triggered my call to the office.

We weren't just launching another conference. We were building a one-stop platform to educate Silicon Valley — and eventually the world — about cloud computing.

Jeremy went to work immediately and wrote a piece titled *What's Cloud Computing?* It became the centerpiece of our event website.

By Monday morning, CloudEXPO was officially announced.

* * *

At the time, I didn't pretend to know exactly how big this would become.

But I had seen this movie before.

When we launched Java Developer's Journal, PowerBuilder was still paying the bills. Java was the experiment. Within a few years, Java grew to ten times the size of PowerBuilder.

And I knew — instinctively — that cloud computing would dwarf Java.

If Java multiplied our business by ten, the cloud would multiply it again.

This wasn't a trend.

It was the next foundation of computing.

And once again, we weren't late.

We were early.

CHAPTER 27
CLOUD EXPO 
JUNE 6-9
NEW YORK CITY
SYS-CON
CloudEXPO
JUNE 6-9
NEW YORK CITY
BIG BOSS?

CNN Breaking News

We had six months.

That was all the time between the Silicon Valley event we had just finished and our June show at the Javits Center in New York City.

Six months to turn momentum into something real.

* * *

Louis finished the artwork for the massive LED billboard mounted on the front of Javits — the one facing Eleventh Avenue, visible from ten blocks away.

Big type.

Bold dates.

CloudEXPO
June 6–9
New York City

We needed photos of it running.

Sales material.
Proof.

So I got in my car, crossed the George Washington Bridge, and drove straight into Manhattan.

I parked near Javits and walked inside.

No badge.
No entourage.
Just me — and a CD in my hand.

* * *

The billboard office was tucked behind the exhibit halls.

Inside sat a man with a thick accent and a half-open pizza box on his desk.

I handed him the artwork.

"Listen," I said. "We have a show here in June. I brought the final graphic. Can you run it on the billboard for ten minutes? I'll go outside, take a few photos, and I'll be out of your way."

He studied me.
Then he said,

"I already got my pizza. Aren't you the pizza delivery man?"

I blinked.

"No," I said. "I'm with SYS-CON."

He leaned back in his chair.

"I don't know who you are," he said. "I have to call SYS-CON."

He picked up the phone.

"There is a pizza delivery man in my office," he said. "He says he knows you."

He turned toward me.

"What is your name?"

I told him.

He put the call on speaker.

Corinna answered.

"This man says he works for you," he said.

There was a pause.

Then Corinna said, without hesitation,
"That's the big boss.
That's the owner of the company."

The man looked at me again.

Longer this time.

Then he nodded.
"Okay," he said. "We will run your billboard."

* * *

Ten minutes later, our show was glowing thirty feet tall on the face of
Javits.

I stood across the street taking photos like a tourist.
Then I got back in my car and drove north.
Mission accomplished.

* * *

That was just the beginning.

I bought every billboard space I could find — including one in Times
Square.

We ran banners inside subway trains.

Huge LED ads at the entrances of the Lincoln and Holland Tunnels.

Radio spots every twenty-two minutes on CBS's 1010 WINS.

Thirty-second commercials on CNBC, from Long Island to New Jersey.

For six straight months, we were everywhere.

You would've thought we were launching new Calvin Klein underwear.

* * *

CloudEXPO New York opened.

Oracle had been our longtime sponsor going back to the Java Developer's Journal days. But within months, the secret was out.

Silicon Valley had heard the word "cloud."

And we were the only game in town.

Every company with a half-built cloud strategy wanted a booth.

Microsoft rolled in massive hardware for its 40×40 booth, glowing with neon-green light behind glass walls.

IBM.
Oracle.
Google.

Startups with deep VC pockets and bigger ambitions.

If you wanted to be someone in Silicon Valley, you were at CloudEXPO.

* * *

The scale was unreal.

Every Fortune 50 company was on our expo floor.

We ran out of space — so we began leasing conference rooms inside our own conference.

Companies were holding their own events inside space we were already renting from the convention center.

That's when I knew we were no longer running an event.

We were running a city.

* * *

Oracle arrived with thirty VIP cars, each wrapped in red Oracle Cloud branding, shuttling executives directly to their booth.

The show floor never slept.

On opening day, we noticed a CNN crew walking the expo floor.

They filmed.

They interviewed attendees.

That night, an eleven-minute segment aired on CNN's evening news — worldwide.

They ran it again.
And again.
For an entire week.

You couldn't buy that kind of exposure for millions of dollars.

* * *

Our keynotes came from places no technology conference had ever reached.

Ira "Gus" Hunt, the CTO of the CIA.

Jill Singer, the CIO of the National Reconnaissance Office.

Cloud computing wasn't a theory anymore.

It was national infrastructure.

And for one week in New York City, it all lived under our roof.

* * *

I remember seeing a tweet.

Someone was asking what was happening in Manhattan. He couldn't find a hotel room anywhere in the city.

Another person replied,

"This week is CloudEXPO in New York."

We had sold out the hotels.

All of them.

* * *

In the middle of the show, Jeremy delivered devastating news.

He had been diagnosed with pancreatic cancer.

He returned to Denmark to begin treatment.

On Twitter, he shared his diagnosis publicly.

Later, Jeremy told us what happened next.

Ten hours after that tweet, his doorbell rang.

He was at his summer house.

Two men in black suits stood outside.

They handed him an envelope.

Inside was a get-well card.

Embossed with the raised seal of the National Reconnaissance Office.

It had been sent from Washington, D.C.

From Jill Singer — the CIO of the NRO.

* * *

That's when it hit me.

This wasn't just a conference anymore.

This was something far bigger than us.

We had arrived early — at least two years ahead of the market.

And for the next twenty years, no serious competitor ever dared to announce a rival event.

They knew our history.

And they knew there was no surviving a fight with momentum like that.

CHAPTER 28

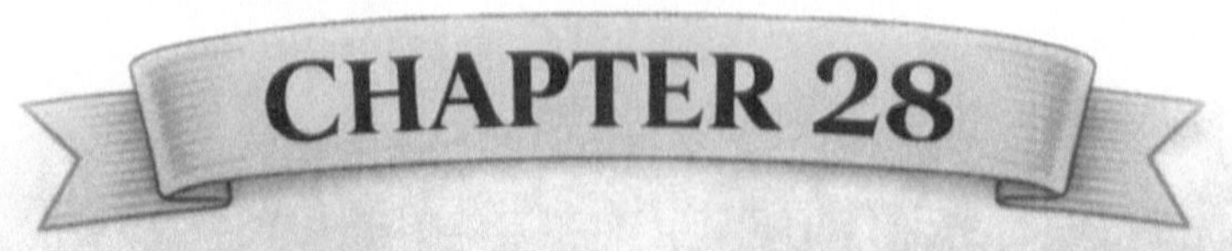

At one of our shows at the Javits Center, Grisha introduced me to a short, chubby man named Shelly.

We spotted him roaming the expo floor, walking booth to booth, handing out business cards and asking companies to attend his event in Las Vegas.

That man was Sheldon Adelson.

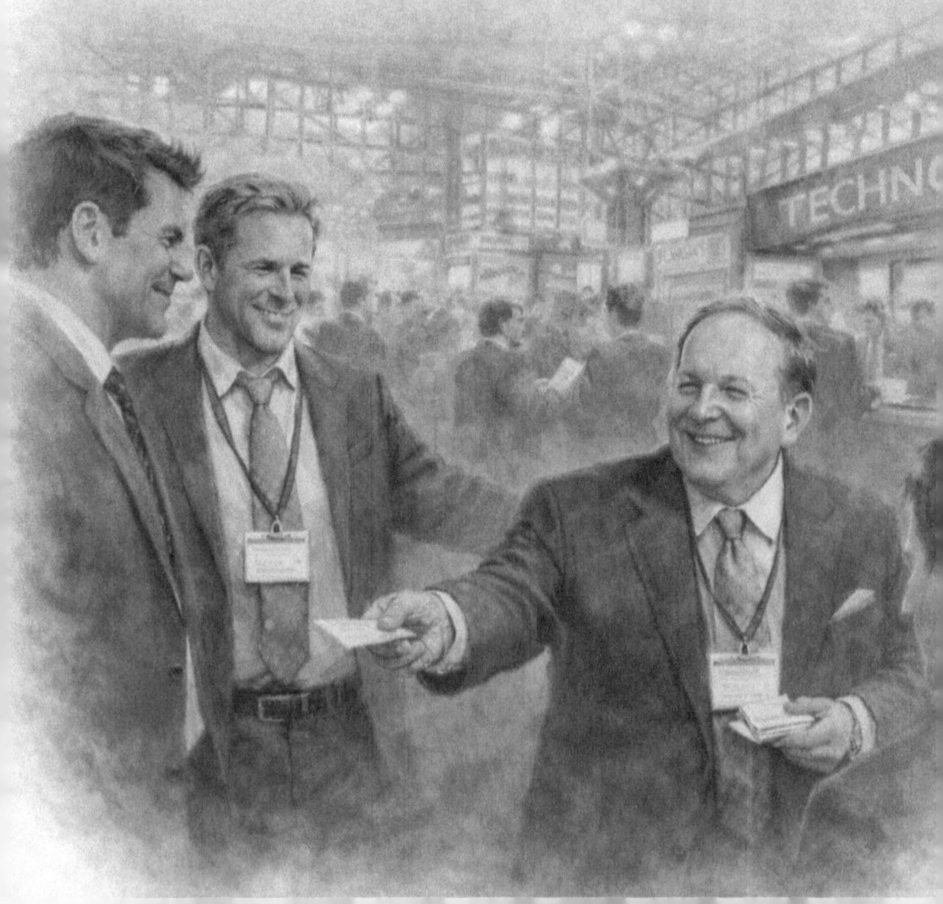

From PC EXPO to CloudEXPO

I hired Grisha Davida in 1998 as President of SYS-CON Events.

By then, Grisha was already a legend in the technology conference world — one of the rare executives whose career bridged the early personal-computer era and the modern enterprise-tech boom.

His reputation had been built long before I met him.

* * *

In 1984, Grisha became the founding president of PC EXPO, working with the show's owner, Ralph Ianuzzi, Sr. Years later, I would discover that his son, Ralph Jr., lived just a few doors from me in Upper Saddle River, New Jersey — one of those small-world coincidences that kept repeating throughout my life.

The personal computer industry was exploding, and PC EXPO quickly became one of the most important technology trade shows in the United States.

Before the Javits Center became its home, PC EXPO was held at the New York Coliseum. There, it brought together volume buyers and sellers of computer hardware, software, and services.

It helped define what a modern technology conference could be — not just booths and brochures, but an ecosystem where an industry learned how to gather.

Grisha played a central role in the show's early growth. Even decades later, historical references and retrospectives still credit him as PC EXPO's founding president.

* * *

After PC EXPO, Grisha came on to build SYS-CON Events with me in the mid-1990s.

Together, we created a conference company focused on emerging technologies.

Under his leadership, we launched dozens of events. Over time, those efforts culminated in CloudEXPO, which debuted in 2008 and went on to become one of the world's largest cloud computing conferences.

In promotional materials, CloudEXPO is sometimes loosely dated to earlier years, reflecting precursor events and the long evolution of the brand.

But its impact became undeniable in the late 2000s, when cloud computing moved from theory into real infrastructure.

Grisha remained actively involved for decades, continuing to appear in CloudEXPO leadership roles and public promotions well into the 2020s.

His career uniquely connected two eras:

the formative years of personal computing

and the rise of cloud and enterprise technology

Few people in the industry could claim both.

Inside SYS-CON, Grisha became the executive backbone of our events business — the steady hand behind our growth as we scaled faster than any of us imagined.

There was one irony I never missed.

When Grisha launched PC EXPO in 1984 — the same year I arrived in the United States — I used to attend the show simply to collect free swag and T-shirts. Enough to last me the entire year.

Years later, I would be running conferences of my own.

And the man who once ran the show I walked into as a broke immigrant would become my president.

At one of our shows at the Javits Center, Grisha introduced me to a short, chubby man named Shelly.

We spotted him roaming the expo floor, walking booth to booth, handing out business cards and asking companies to attend his event in Las Vegas.

That man was Sheldon Adelson.

At the time, he was just another promoter hustling the floor.

But his Las Vegas event would soon become COMDEX — short for Computer Dealers Expo — one of the most influential trade shows in the history of the personal computer industry.

* * *

COMDEX quickly became the centerpiece of the tech calendar.

By the late 1980s and throughout the 1990s, Fall COMDEX in Las Vegas grew into the world's largest trade show, often drawing more than 200,000 attendees at its peak.

Product launches happened there.

Partnerships were formed there.

Entire sectors of the computing industry were shaped on that floor.

Adelson and his partners later sold The Interface Group — including COMDEX and its related shows — to Japan's SoftBank Corporation, led by Masayoshi Son, for approximately $862 to $890 million.

Adelson's personal share was reportedly well over $500 million.

I met him when he was still walking booth to booth with business cards in his hand.

* * *

That's how this industry worked back then.

Everyone started on the floor.

Everyone I met at the top, I first saw walking the floor.

Chapter 29

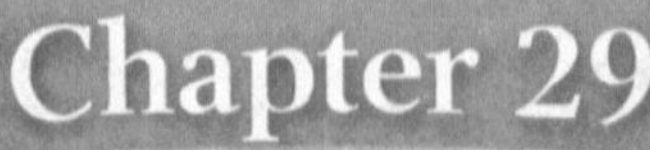

The $1,200 Bottle I Opened the Day the Iraq War Started

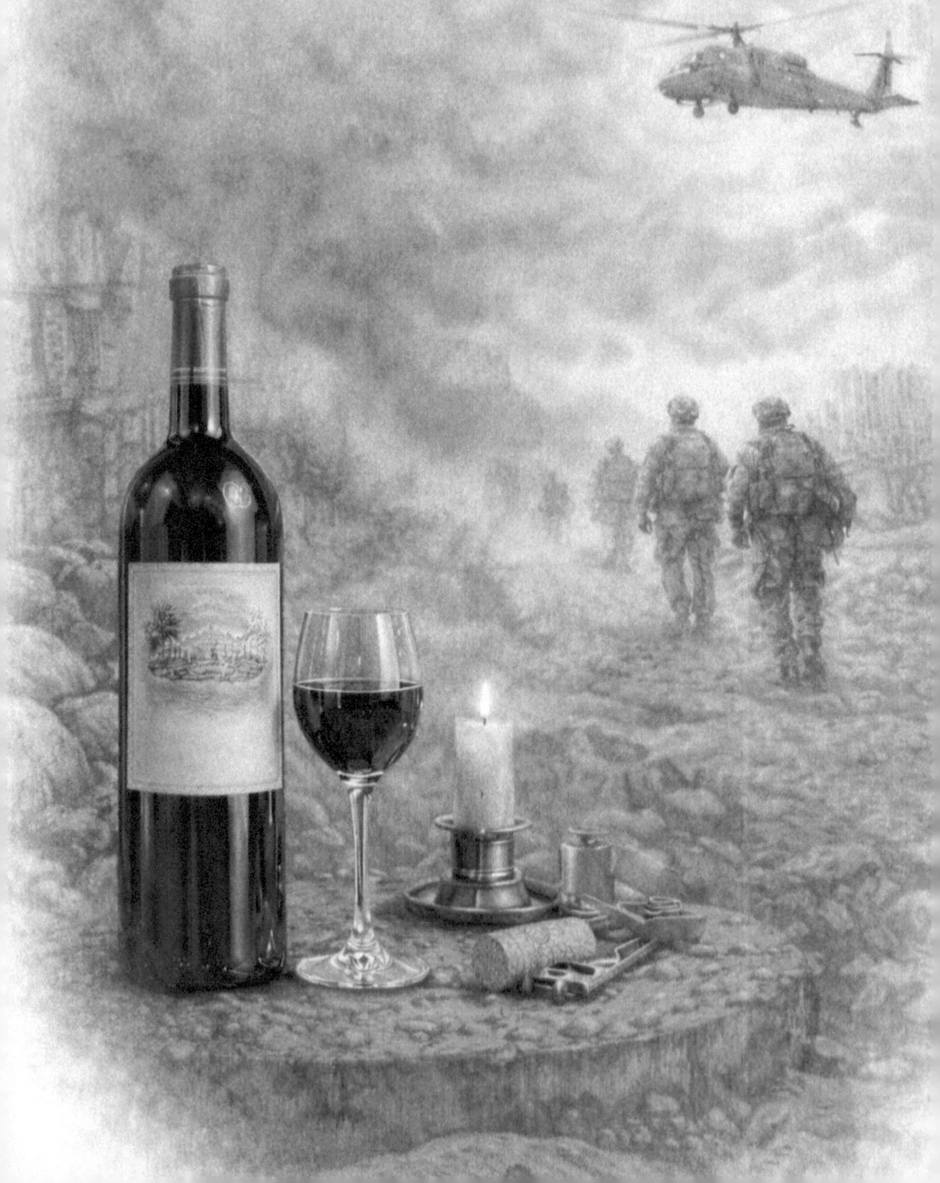

Château Lafite Rothschild

We held our East Coast event in Boston that year — the same week as LinuxWorld.

It was March 17, 2003.

Monday for setup.

Tuesday through Friday for the show.

Four days inside the Boston Convention Center, with IDG's Linux-World upstairs and our Web Services Edge conference running below.

But something felt wrong.

The air wasn't competitive or energetic — it was uneasy.

Outside the building, the country was bracing for war.

Inside, everyone felt it.

Iraq was coming.

That year, we also did something no one else was doing.

We streamed live from the expo floor.

At the time, it was revolutionary. No conferences were broadcasting in real time — not audio, not video. We were doing it live, directly from the show floor, using Macromedia's Flash Player.

We were a Macromedia partner, publishing five magazines for them. Because of that relationship, they shared an early beta version of their live-streaming technology with us — software very few people in the world had ever touched.

It ran on RTMP — Real-Time Messaging Protocol — designed to make low-latency live video possible over the internet.

For the first time, people who weren't in the building could see what was happening inside it — as it happened.

That same technology would later shape the earliest era of online video and influence platforms that came years afterward.

At the time, we weren't thinking about history.

We just knew we were doing something no one else was doing yet.

That breakthrough sparked another idea.

I told Robert that online gaming was about to explode — and when it did, it wouldn't belong only to kids anymore. It would become a real industry.

We decided to be first.

That idea became CyberGamer — our first consumer magazine and our first step outside the enterprise technology world.

It was a risk.
But it worked.

Later, we expanded even further — launching International Yacht Vacations & Charters, distributed worldwide on newsstands, followed by Private Jet Charters. Different audiences. Different lifestyles.

But driven by the same instinct that had always guided me:

See what's coming — and move before everyone else does.

By then, Roger Strukhoff — a close friend — was at the show.

Roger had spent years at IDG, and through him I suddenly found myself face-to-face with someone I never expected to meet.

Pat McGovern. IDG's founder.

I was standing at our live-streaming booth when I saw Roger walking toward me with him. We shook hands, took a few photos, and within seconds Pat began asking questions — not polite ones, but genuinely curious ones.

How does it work? Who's watching? Where does the signal go?

Pat preferred to be called the Chairman.

That day, I met the Chairman.

McGovern was a rare combination — deeply intelligent, intensely curious, and entirely self-made.

A Boston native and MIT graduate, he had launched Computerworld in 1964, long before most people even understood what a computer was.

That single newspaper grew into IDG.

At its peak, the company operated in more than one hundred countries, publishing titles like PC World, Macworld, and InfoWorld, while building IDC into one of the most influential technology research firms in the world.

He built it all from nothing.
A self-made billionaire.

And there we were — standing on a noisy expo floor — talking about live video streaming before almost anyone else believed it mattered.

What always fascinated me about Pat wasn't his wealth — it was how little it seemed to change him.

He knew people throughout IDG by name. At the annual Christmas party, he personally handed out bonus checks, greeting employees one by one — always by their first names.

For a man worth billions, he was disarmingly unsophisticated about everyday life.

Once, needing help with a banking issue, he simply walked into a local branch and stood in line like everyone else.

When he reached the teller window and explained what he needed, the staff froze.

They were staring at a man whose account balance approached a billion dollars — waiting patiently at the counter.

Pat was also famously frugal.

For years, his official residence was a modest rental townhouse near the New Hampshire border — Live Free or Die.

On weekends, he would drive up, open his mail, pay his rent and utility bills, and then return to his Boston mansion.

It saved him a substantial amount in taxes.

To Pat, it wasn't clever.

It was just practical.

* * *

By the time we met in Boston, Pat already knew our reputation.

Not long afterward, we licensed the LinuxWorld name from IDG and launched LinuxWorld Magazine.

But that Boston show itself turned into a disaster.

On the second day of the event, President George W. Bush launched the Iraq War.

The convention center emptied almost instantly — on a scale I wouldn't see again until COVID.

I left Grisha behind to manage whatever remained of the final days.

I took Carmen and her two sales managers, loaded everyone into my car, and drove straight back to our office in New Jersey.

Somewhere along the way, in Greenwich, Connecticut, I pulled off the highway.

I stopped at Valbella — one of my favorite Italian restaurants.

I asked to be seated in the wine cellar.

I ordered lunch.

And I ordered a $1,200 bottle of Château Lafite Rothschild.

Because sometimes, when the world collapses in real time,

you don't panic.

You pause.

You drink something exceptional.

Then you figure out what comes next.

Chapter 30

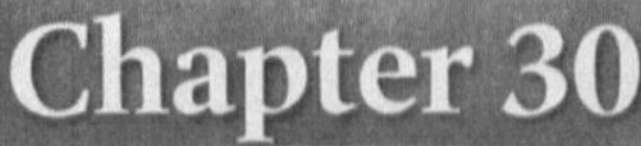

Bill Coleman and *the* Chairman's Wife

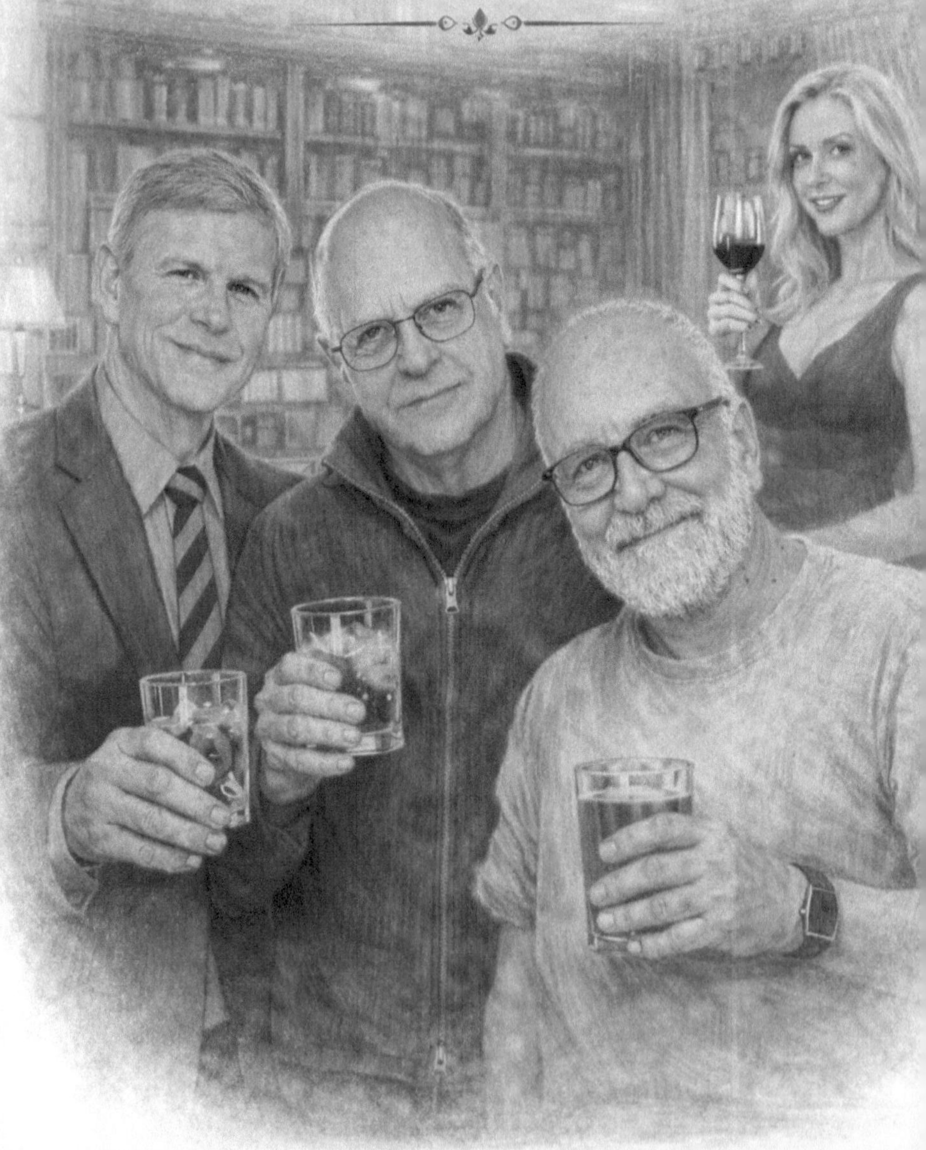

Bill Coleman and the Chairman's Wife

B efore we moved our events to the Javits Center the following year, the Roosevelt Hotel in Manhattan was our launch pad. It was where we tested our ideas, built momentum, and figured out whether a subject had legs to become a full-scale event. These were essentially our pilot shows—smaller events that often went on to have a few years of life.

One evening, at the end of the first day of one of those events, Roger and I were at the hotel bar having drinks with Bill Coleman—the "B" in BEA Systems. The company's name came from the first initials of its three founders: Bill Coleman, Ed Scott, and Alfred Chuang. The three executives had started BEA Systems in 1995, and by then their company was one of the most talked-about names in enterprise software.

The opening keynote that day was delivered by Scott Guthrie, the Executive Vice President of Microsoft's Cloud + AI Group.

He led Azure, AI services, Dynamics 365, Power Platform, Visual Studio, VS Code, GitHub, .NET, and more. A Microsoft veteran since 1997 and a key architect of .NET and early Azure, he helped drive the company's cloud dominance under Satya Nadella.

Of course, we published *.NET Developer's Journal* for Scott and Microsoft.

Everyone in my company had a clear role during our events. I didn't. I wasn't representing the business, and I rarely looked the part of a host. I showed up in my usual casual attire—ripped jeans, worn-out sneakers, and a haircut and shave I'd skipped for a few months. I wasn't there on official company duty.

Next to Roger, Bill, and me was a group from one of our sponsors, enjoying the end of the first day. They were cheerful and a little loud. One of the men pointed across the bar at Carmen and said, "Check this out—that woman is really hot."

His colleague quickly interrupted him. "Stop. That's the chairman's wife."

The first guy looked stunned. "No kidding? Is that Jeremy's wife?"

Jeremy was our conference chair. I had put him in the role, and he delivered it beautifully in his polished Oxford accent. But in casual conversations he had a habit of introducing himself as the company's chairman. At one point, Tim O'Reilly, thinking Jeremy was the real deal, flew him to Texas to discuss a partnership. That meeting must have ended faster than any other.

Roger and I had been listening to the whole exchange just inches away. I turned toward the group and said, "She's not Jeremy's wife. She's my wife."

That turned out to be the biggest joke they'd heard all day. They burst out laughing. One of them walked over to Carmen and asked, "Excuse me, Carmen—who is your husband?"

She pointed across the bar. "That man over there, standing next to Roger."

The executives from the sponsor company looked genuinely shocked. For the rest of the evening, they went out of their way to show me respect as "Carmen's husband," but they still had no idea who I actually was.

By then, Bill, Roger, and I had more than enough drinks. We helped Bill to the elevator, said our goodnights, and headed back to our rooms.

Bill Coleman was a genuinely good man. During the dot-com bubble, his net worth approached a billion dollars. He was also active in philanthropy, particularly in education and youth programs. Through the Coleman Family Foundation, he supported initiatives focused on leadership development, college access, and opportunities for underserved students pursuing careers in technology and business.

Alfred and I didn't get along, though—Alfred, as in the "A" in BEA Systems. Toward the peak of the dot-com bubble, we practically ruled Silicon Valley. Every software company needed magazine publishers. We were their voice to customers.

I covered both sides of the bloody app server war: IBM and BEA.

I was publishing the *BEA WebLogic Developer's Journal* while also publishing the *IBM WebSphere Developer's Journal*—both on newsstands worldwide.

Then Alfred made a deal behind our backs, and Jim Fawcette launched a competing title with BEA's support.

Within a few months, we had effectively put both BEA Systems and Fawcette Technical Publications out of the game.

The final issue of my *WebLogic Developer's Journal* carried the headline:

"Is BEA DOA?"

With that issue, we essentially handed the application server narrative to IBM.

In April 2008, Oracle acquired BEA Systems for about $8.5 billion, bringing the company's influential WebLogic platform into Oracle's enterprise software stack. Around the same time, the bank in Washington, D.C., sold Fawcette Technical Publications to 1105 Media.

Chapter 31

James Gosling and Rudy Giuliani

S cott McNealy's lawyers were not businessmen, and his PR team seemed better suited to staging Bay Area homes for sale. They were useless.

One day I received a phone call from a Sun Microsystems lawyer. He said that "Java" in *Java Developer's Journal* was a registered trademark of Sun Microsystems and that we could not use it in our magazine title. I thought, *Fuck them.* I went over to production and told Jim and Alex we were changing the next issue's logo to JDJ. Problem solved. I told the production team that Scott's lawyers could go fuck themselves.

I hate stupidity. And this was very stupid. The McNealy lawyer pissed me off so much that I went back to production and told the designers to announce the JDJ Edge Conference & Expo right on the cover of JDJ. All our readers were already referring to *Java Developer's Journal* as JDJ, *PowerBuilder Developer's Journal* as PBDJ, *ColdFusion Developer's Journal* as CFDJ, and so on.

We never got a phone call from Jeremy Allaire's lawyers reminding us that ColdFusion was their trademark, or from Sybase telling us that PowerBuilder was theirs. In fact, we published PBDJ—our first magazine—which we printed for two decades, and it became the foundation of a company that lasted more than twenty years, alongside twenty other titles we launched along the way. Scott McNealy's lawyers, who apparently had nothing better to do, decided to harass us. To hell with them.

Even though my events executives, Grisha Davida and Cathy Walters, were on top of their game, JDJ Edge became my personal baby.

We booked James Gosling—the creator of Java and a Sun Microsystems executive—as the opening keynote for our JDJ Edge event at the Javits Center in New York. What were those lawyers going to do—trademark Gosling's photo too? Fire him? To hell with them.

***

Fast forward to seven days after 9/11. Like the rest of the world, we were trying to get our bearings. We had a show coming up at the Javits, but the convention center had been turned into a triage center for the World Trade Center disaster.

I asked Grisha to call Jack Buttine. Everyone bought their trade show insurance from him. He was a specialist in trade show insurance, exhibitor liability, and event-related coverage. They assured us we were fully insured—against terrorism, acts of God, fire, earthquakes, anything.

What they didn't realize was that our policy had been written with AIG, and Hank Greenberg was not the kind of insurance partner you could trust. I covered that in another chapter in sufficient detail.

***

There was no discussion of doing a trade show in New York City—or anywhere in the world—so soon after what we had just lived through.

We held a management meeting, decided to cancel the event, and began refunding the attendees who called in.

Then we received a phone call from Rudy Giuliani's office. The woman on the line explained that the city needed every bit of economic activity it could generate. The mayor was asking us not to cancel our event.

We rescheduled the venue to the New York Hilton on Sixth Avenue. It became the only trade show held anywhere in the world during the year after 9/11.

There were no flights. James Gosling flew from San Francisco to London, and from London to New York, just to deliver his opening keynote.

Selling an Island to Jimmy Buffett

Selling an Island to Jimmy Buffett

L ast week I stopped by my local Uncle Giuseppe's supermarket. On weekends, there's a one-man band who wanders the aisles singing while you shop. You hear him long before you see him.

That day, he was singing Margaritaville.

He was good — really good. Honestly, he could have passed for one of Jimmy Buffett's cover-band singers.

I finally found him in the fresh foods aisle and asked,

"Who's that supposed to be?"

He said,

"Jimmy Buffett."

I replied,
"I sold my house to him. He's sleeping in my bed."

The singer looked at my Lieutenant Columbo outfit — wrinkled jacket, three-month-old beard — and laughed so hard he skipped a few lines of the song.

Then he looked at me and said,
"You know Jimmy Buffett died last year, right?"

That's how I learned the news.

From a karaoke singer in an Italian supermarket.

***

Two decades earlier, I had returned from my Fourth of July trip to Bodrum, staying at the Divan Palmira with the boys — Grisha, Jeremy, Alex, and Robert — and went straight back to work Monday morning, because apparently I believed vacations cure everything.

I stopped by the office bathroom and discovered something deeply unsettling in my underwear — a shade of red best described as Cabernet Sauvignon, 1998. Bold. Full-bodied. Absolutely not recommended before breakfast.

Five seconds later, I was no longer a brave entrepreneur.
I was a man calling his wife.

Carmen drove me across the George Washington Bridge to Columbia Presbyterian Hospital while I sat in complete silence, wondering whether this was how my story ended — bleeding internally on a weekday, before lunch, with meetings still on my calendar.

It was a depressing situation.

While we waited for test results that Friday, Carmen decided I needed fresh air — or at least distance from New Jersey. She put me on a JetBlue flight back to our place in Florida at 3001 NE 36th Street in Lighthouse Point. I still have that address on my driver's license.

On Saturday afternoon we drove to Shooters Waterfront — a lively dockside restaurant right on the Fort Lauderdale Intracoastal.

It was a beautiful day. Boats drifted by. The sun sparkled on the water.

Everyone looked healthy.
Suspiciously healthy.

I sat there with a beer and very gloomy thoughts.

Finally, I said,
"Carmen... let's go buy a boat."

She didn't laugh.

That should have been my first warning.

We drove straight to MarineMax on Federal Highway just before closing time. A salesman greeted us.

"Hi, I'm Peter Quintal."

We told him we were there to buy a boat. He walked us down the dock, showing model after model tied neatly in the water.

When we reached the very end, I stopped, pointed, and said,

"Peter... that's it? I've seen bigger Sea Rays."

He didn't blink.

"We have a 58-foot Aft Cabin in Tampa," he said. "We can bring it."

Perfect.

I paid the deposit that afternoon and bought a 58-foot Sea Ray Aft Cabin for $1.2 million — about $2.38 million in today's money — the very same day I was still waiting for my medical test results.

When we returned to New Jersey and went back to work, my new boat was delivered and tied up outside my house — because nothing says responsible medical recovery like purchasing a floating apartment.

I told the boys I had bought a beautiful brand-new boat with three staterooms.

Now it needed a name.

Alex designed the logo.

By the time I flew back to my Florida home to see it for the first time, the name was already painted on the aft of the boat:

FuYacht — Lighthouse Point.

***

The following Friday, Carmen and I anxiously flew back to Florida to see my stunning new purchase.

I hired Paul Turner as my captain. Paul lived at Lighthouse Point Marina, just around the corner.

Carmen set up her laptop at the living-room table of FuYacht and jumped straight into work, as if she were sitting in her office back in New Jersey.

I turned to our captain and said,

"Captain Paul, we've never been to the Bahamas. Can you take us there?"

He smiled. The weather was perfect — the ocean calm like a glass mirror.

"I never leave home without my passport," Paul said. "If you both have yours, we can leave right now."

Carmen pulled her passport from her handbag.

I had mine in my jacket pocket.

Done.

FuYacht was equipped with a full satellite navigation system — a Raymarine array radar integrated with autopilot, with a range of forty-eight miles.

From the Lighthouse Point inlet, we could already see an island glowing on the radar screen — a place we would later learn was exactly where Paul was planning to take us.

Captain Paul hollered from the upper deck,

"We're here — welcome to the Bahamas!"

I ran upstairs to the third deck. Carmen joined me.

We stared at the land ahead.

"Captain Paul," I said, "where are we? This can't be the Bahamas. This is a tiny deserted island — the kind you see in cartoons with one palm tree."

He smiled.

"There are more than seven hundred islands in the Bahamas," he said. "This one is Cat Cay. It's a private island."

Then he added casually,

"I need to run over to immigration, get your passports stamped, and secure permits before you're allowed to step ashore."

A few minutes later he disappeared down the dock in a golf cart — leaving Carmen and me standing on the deck, staring at our very own cartoon island.

When he returned, he said,

"Get in the golf cart. Let me give you an island tour."

The tour lasted about thirty seconds.

End to end, the entire island was barely a quarter mile long — smaller than thirty acres.

But then I saw turkeys, chickens, tiny baby chicks, and roosters singing their proud cock-a-doodle-doo.

Suddenly the island didn't feel small at all.

It reminded me of my mother's village, Osmaneli, where we spent our childhood summers.

***

I was on my BlackBerry texting with Levent as we arrived at David and his wife's house.

Captain Paul opened the door and walked straight in — no knocking, no hello.

Suddenly we were standing in the middle of David's living room.

During our introductions, David mentioned they lived in Cherry Hill, Pennsylvania.

I asked,

"Do you work for that international company based there?"

He looked surprised.

"Yes. How did you know?"

"Well," I said, "that's the only massive corporation in that town with a global headquarters."

At the same time I texted Levent:

You won't believe this — I just met a man from your company on a deserted island in the Bahamas, and now I'm standing in his living room.

Then I sent David's full name.

Levent replied instantly:

"He's the worldwide CEO of the company I work for. How did you run into him?"

I looked at David and said,

"My friend Levent runs your Turkey operation. He's very upset about the Saudi Arabia curveball you threw at him yesterday. He didn't think it was fair. He sends his regards — and says you need a stronger management team in Turkey."

David froze.

I continued,

"He accepted the CEO position at your biggest competitor this morning."

That's how David found out.

From me.

On a tiny private island in the Bahamas.

What a small world.

***

Carmen and I have fond memories of Cat Cay.

We eventually bought a property there.

Our next-door neighbor was Wayne Huizenga.

I cooked many menemen breakfasts for Wayne and his wife, Marti. We were so close as neighbors that if you stretched your arms out, you could almost touch both houses at the same time.

Marti once gave Wayne a $75 million yacht for his birthday — Floridian, previously owned by Greg Norman.

Barry Gibb of the Bee Gees also had a place on Cat Cay with his wife, Linda. During the band's peak years they spent a lot of time in South Florida, and Cat Cay was one of those quiet islands where celebrities could disappear for a while.

I invited Levent to Cat Cay once. We were driving to the golf course when we ran into Sandra MacMillan.

She said, "Hi Levent. Hi Fuat."

We replied, "Hi Sandra."

Sandra is one of the heirs to the Cargill giant. Her father was John H. "Hugh" MacMillan III of the Cargill family.

Levent turned to me and said,

"The Turkish president would wait six months to get an appointment with Sandra."

That weekend, the three of us were the only people on the entire island.

Talking about the S&L crisis — Charles Keating had a home on Cat Cay before my time. Richard Nixon, Bebe Rebozo, and John McCain were frequent guests on the island.

But while I was living there, one day a homeless-looking man appeared. He bought half a dozen homes, tore them down, and built himself a beautiful spread. We were invited to his housewarming party.

At one point Carmen's father locked himself in the guest bathroom and couldn't get out. We ended up rescuing him through the tiny bathroom window.

The man who had just bought half the neighborhood was John Devaney.

John Devaney is a Wall Street investor known for founding United Capital Markets. He built a multibillion-dollar hedge fund trading distressed debt and mortgage securities during the credit boom of the 1990s and early 2000s. His firm suffered major losses during the 2008 financial crisis and eventually shut down, but Devaney remained active in distressed investing and credit markets afterward.

***

During my divorce from Carmen, I put our home on the market.

I was living in Turkey at the time, staying in my mother's village house, sleeping on a thin mattress on the living-room floor.

One afternoon my phone rang.

I answered.

The voice on the other end said,

"I'm so-and-so. I want to buy your property on Cat Cay."

I replied,

"Yes, it's for sale."

There was a pause.

Then he said,

"You don't know who I am?"

I said,

"I'm Fuat Kircaali. Do you know who I am?"

The lawyers handled the paperwork, and I sold our beautiful private-island home.

Weeks later, I learned who the buyer actually was.

Jimmy Buffett.

Apparently, even my divorce needed a soundtrack.

And somewhere, in some supermarket aisle, someone is still singing Margaritaville.

Fade out.

CHAPTER 33

Dick Cheney invited us to a dinner
with President George W. Bush and Laura.
Carmen and I attended.

Dick Cheney
Vice President of the United States

May 1, 2002

Fuat Kircaali
28 Arrowshard Dr.
Upper Saddle River, NJ 07458-1301

Dear Fuat,

Vice President
Vice President of the United States

Dinner With a President

D ICK CHENEY

May 1, 2002

Fuat Kircaali
28 Arrowhead Dr.
Upper Saddle River, NJ 07458-1301

Dear Fuat,

I write to invite you to join the President and Mrs. Bush for a private dinner here in Washington, D.C. on June 19th and also to ask you to serve as a representative of Upper Saddle River, New Jersey at the President's Dinner.

In fact, a special place of honor has already been reserved for you to recognize your steadfast support of President Bush.

Enclosed are your official invitation and your R.S.V.P. Reply Card. If for any reason you cannot be here on the 19th, the President and I still want to honor you for your service to our party and your past support. So if you cannot attend, please accept the honor of becoming an Honorary Co-Chairman of The President's Dinner.

As you know, The President's Dinner is traditionally the kickoff for the fall campaign season and the cornerstone of the President's personal effort to maintain and expand our very slim Republican majority in the

House and to regain our Republican majority in the U.S. Senate.

***

Electing a Republican majority in the U.S. Senate and expanding our Republican majority in the House is perhaps the most important service you can provide President Bush at this time.

That is why I hope you will attend The President's Dinner or, if you cannot attend, that you will serve as an Honorary Co-Chairman of The Dinner and help us maintain and increase our Republican majority in the U.S. House and regain our majority in the U.S. Senate.

Please don't delay in returning your R.S.V.P. Card to let us know you will be coming for dinner and that we can count on your support during the 2002 election.

Together President Bush and our Republican leadership in the U.S. Senate and House of Representatives have accomplished a great deal. We have cut taxes, reformed education, rallied the nation to confront and fight terrorism both here and abroad and fulfilled our promise to bring compassionate conservatism to Washington.

We could not have accomplished these goals without your support. And we will not finish the job without Republican majorities in both the House and the Senate.

Thank you for your continued support. We hope you will attend The President's Dinner.

Sincerely,

Dick Cheney
Vice President of the United States

ACT III — EVERYTHING THAT COMES WITH IT

Success doesn't just bring rewards.

It brings weight.

Every decision echoes longer. Every mistake costs more. And every win attracts consequences no one warns you about.

This act is not about building — it's about living with what was built. The marriages, the divorces, the courtrooms, the contradictions, and the quiet moments when the noise finally fades.

The price of momentum is that eventually, it demands to be paid.

And it always collects.

CHAPTER 34

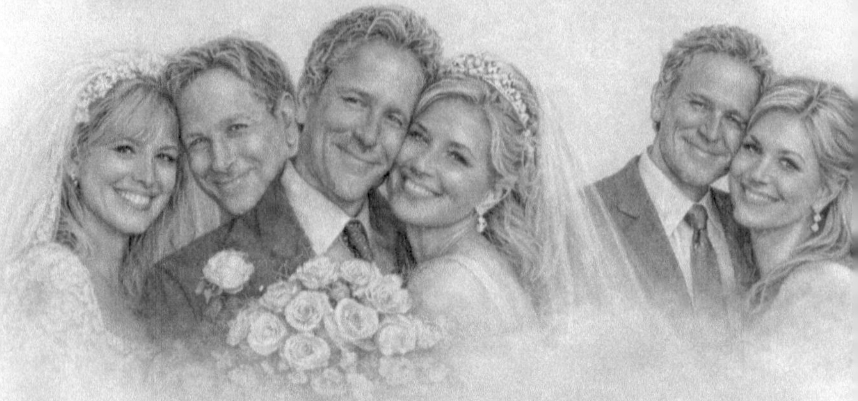

All my ex-wives lived on the same street. I did grocery shopping for all homes.

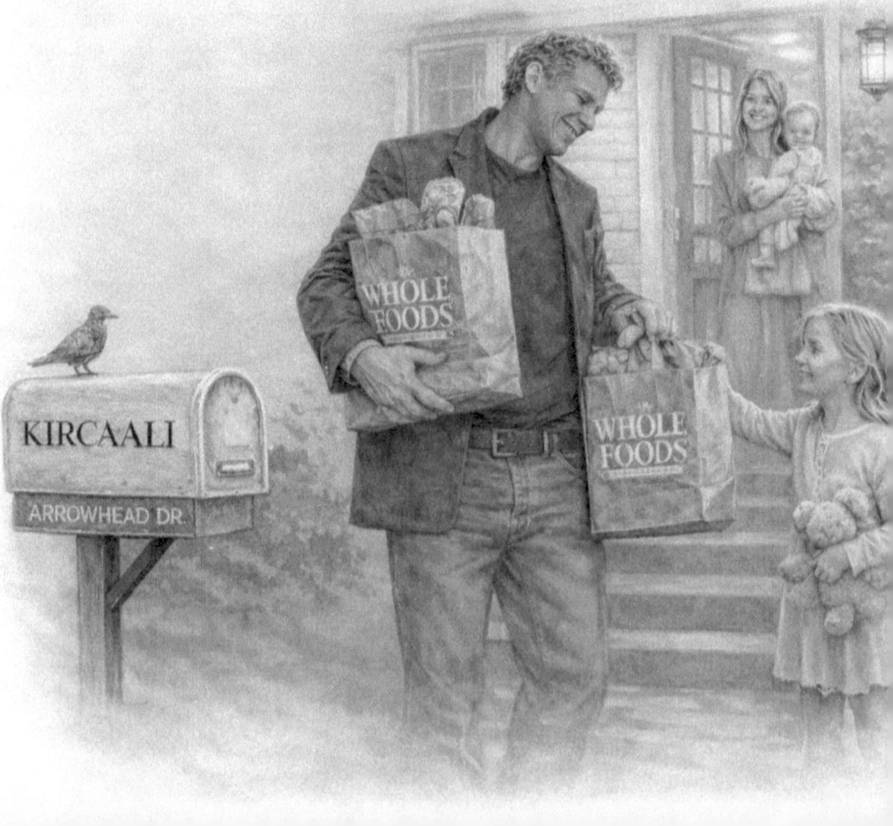

Ten Years, Five Wives

I n 1985, while working at the Movado Watch Company, I met my first wife. What immediately caught my attention was that she was not only very pretty, but also incredibly hardworking—almost as driven as I was. I was twenty-six; she was nineteen. We became good friends first, long before either of us thought about turning it into a relationship.

Before one long weekend, she called me at home. She said the upcoming Fourth of July weekend was five days long and suggested we go somewhere. She wanted to see if we could find cheap tickets to Los Angeles. I found a $178 round-trip flight to Las Vegas instead and suggested we rent a car there and drive to L.A. That became the plan.

We rented a car, arrived in L.A., and spent a wonderful time roller-skating on Venice Beach and taking pictures along Hollywood Boulevard. On July 4, we drove back to Las Vegas to catch our early-morning flight to New York the next day. As we drove along the Strip, we noticed the neon lights of the Candlelight Wedding Chapel. Curious, we walked in.

The man behind the reception desk—who reminded me of a clerk at a cheap highway motel—looked at us and asked, "Are you lovebirds here to get married?" We weren't lovebirds; we were just good friends. We both laughed. Half-joking, I said maybe we should get married. It would certainly be memorable to do it on the Fourth of July. Somehow, we both said yes.

Within minutes, he produced a fake priest and two Mexican witnesses and offered us a full-service package. Just like that, we were married.

When we landed at Newark Airport the next day, we looked at each other and said, well, I guess we're husband and wife now. Maybe we should live together.

After work, we went back to my studio apartment on Bergenline Avenue in Union City, New Jersey. That's how my first marriage started—no grand plan, no dramatic proposal, just a small apartment and two people figuring things out. The rent was $500 a month, which felt manageable at the time.

When I finally quit my slave job at the Movado Watch Company in New York City and landed a new one at United Weight Control in Englewood Cliffs, my salary jumped from $20,000 to $50,000 a year. Overnight, I felt rich. Naturally, we decided it was time to buy a place.

After nearly a year of researching mortgages—just enough to make us feel confident and slightly dangerous—we finally bought a townhouse in Jersey City, at 46 Holly Street. When the mortgage payments started, reality wasted no time showing up. After the check went to the bank each month, there wasn't much left for anything else. Still, we told ourselves this was adulthood. This was what being responsible was supposed to feel like.

Around that same time, my first marriage was quietly coming apart, just as the earliest seeds of SYS-CON Media were beginning to take root.

When I came back from my three-month army boot camp, I found out Marilyn had left. She wanted another child and a different kind of life—the kind where she could take her son and daughter to school every morning and center everything around family. I wasn't there yet. Between the pressure at work and the constant financial stress, I could barely keep my own head above water. I couldn't give her what she wanted, and she knew it. So she left. After that, I didn't hear from her for almost two years.

The very next Monday, I was back at my desk at Rhône-Poulenc, trying to pretend my personal life hadn't just imploded. Then a striking young woman walked past my cubicle, and for reasons I still don't fully understand, I chased after her.

"Excuse me—what's your name?"

"Carmen."

I didn't hesitate.

"Carmen, I'm going to marry you."

That didn't go over well. She reported me to Human Resources for harassment. I later learned she was married. The end result was three months of mandatory "harassment in the workplace" classes, twice a week after work—a humbling, uncomfortable lesson I earned the hard way.

* * *

I'll fill in the exact years later, as they relate to my business story, but about ten years after we met, I married her in a lavish ceremony at Cipriani on 42nd Street in Manhattan. It was an unforgettable night—so extravagant, in fact, that I sometimes joke it may have cost more than Jennifer Lopez's wedding at the same venue.

That was my second marriage, as we know it.

So what came next?

Ten years into our marriage, one morning I woke up, walked into Carmen's corner office at 135 Chestnut Ridge Road in Montvale, New Jersey, closed the door, sat down, and said:

"I want a baby."

She looked at me, surprised.

"You want what?"

"I want a baby."

Carmen leaned back, stared at me for a moment, and then said:

"You're forty-nine years old. You want to be changing diapers at fifty?"

She shook her head.

"I've been there, done that, got the T-shirt. No more diapers for me."

I left her office feeling like a disappointed kid.

* * *

I walked straight to the production department, where Alex, Louis, Abe, Tammy, and a few other designers were working.

I looked at them and said:

"Guys, I want a baby—but Carmen doesn't."

They all stopped and looked at me.

"How am I supposed to have a baby?"

Louis broke the silence.

"Hey, boss," he said. "You can find a new wife online. Go create a profile on Match.com. You'll meet someone who actually wants to have a baby."

The idea stuck.

I couldn't bring myself to tell Carmen I wanted a divorce. She would have killed me—at least emotionally.

So instead, I did the unthinkable.

I created an online dating profile, met someone, and she became pregnant with my baby.

That stretch of my life was complicated in ways I didn't fully appreciate at the time.

Marilyn lived on Rolling Ridge Road in Upper Saddle River. Carmen lived just behind her, on Arrowhead Drive. And the baby's mother ended up on the same street as Marilyn, just across the way. None of them needed to know exactly where the others lived. At the time, I told myself that keeping those boundaries was simply practical.

I remember stopping at the A&P—what's now a Whole Foods—and buying groceries for three different households in a single trip. It felt efficient, almost orderly, even though my life was anything but.

I took Marilyn's daughter to school in the mornings. I stayed close to my newborn baby. And I was still married to, and living with, Carmen.

From the outside, it probably made no sense. From the inside, I convinced myself it did—until I got caught.

Carmen found out. She filed for divorce. And just like that, my daughter's mother became wife number three.

So, in a nutshell, those were my first three marriages.

My fourth and fifth were borderline annulments—nothing to see there.

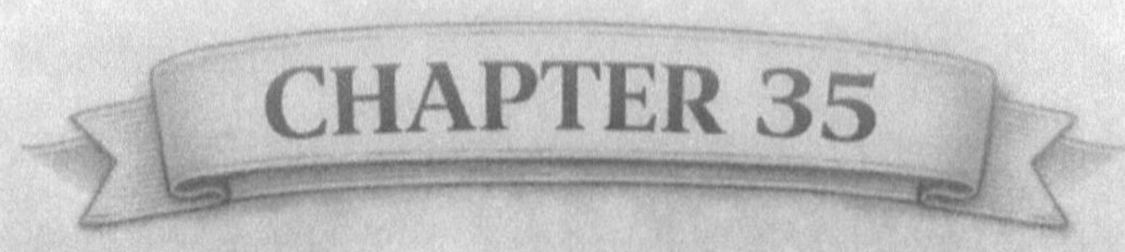

CHAPTER 35

"Your Honor, may I approach the bench?"

She looked annoyed,

"What, Mr. Kircaali?"

In a voice loud enough for the entire courtroom to hear, I said

"Now that we're divorzed,
may I take you out to dinner?"

I was escorted out of the courtroom.

I Asked My Divorce Judge Out

When Carmen joined me on this business adventure in 1994, there was no roadmap — no visibility into the future and absolutely no guarantee it would lead anywhere.

She jumped in anyway.

She carried her share of the weight, pushing through the growing pains of a startup that didn't even know what it was yet.

I was genuinely impressed.

* * *

We got married ten years later.

And divorced twenty years later.

* * *

At the time, she lived with her parents in South Plainfield. Every morning she got up early, drove to Jersey City, walked into our home office with total professionalism, and dove straight into a mountain of work that somehow managed to grow every single day.

When I showed up one morning with the first batch of subscription cards and spread them across the desk in front of her, she quit her day job on the spot. No hesitation. I was the cautious one.

I had a mortgage, and all the money so far existed only in theory. I couldn't afford to quit yet.

So every morning, I drove from my townhouse to my day job, while she drove to that same townhouse — our first office and, unofficially, our headquarters.

That brings me to the most remarkable thing about Carmen.

From the moment she quit her job to join this startup — and through more than thirty years of knowing her — she never once brought up money.

Not once.

We never talked about it. Ever.

She had bills, a car payment, rent, and a baby daughter at home, yet she never asked:

"How much are you going to pay me?"

Two decades later, when she filed for divorce, I had a bulletproof prenuptial agreement.

Both lawyers agreed on that.

Legally, I didn't owe her a dime.

Still, I told the attorneys:

"Listen. You both drafted this agreement ten years ago, each representing one of us. But Carmen was with me from day one. She worked as hard as I did. It's only fair we split everything equally."

The night the divorce was finalized, I heard she threw a massive divorce party at my mansion in Upper Saddle River — the house I left for her and moved on from.

It was a brand-new French-style home.

Eight thousand square feet.

A matching swimming pool.

A movie theater.

A wine cellar.

His-and-hers bedroom suites.

I even designed the pool myself.

I should also mention this:

On the final day of our divorce, the judge threw me out of the court-room.

She never liked me.

From the very first hearing, every time she saw my face, she'd say:

"Mr. Kircaali, you don't have to come to your hearings in person. You can call in from *Bodrum*, which you seem to be living in full-time."

Carmen immediately jumped in.

"I don't want to come either."

The judge replied:

"You should appear in person."

* * *

On the day we received our golden divorce seal, the judge and both lawyers were arguing about appraisers.

They wanted to send people to value every property we owned in New

Jersey and Florida.

My lawyer wanted his appraiser.

Her lawyer wanted his.

I raised my hand.

"Your Honor, give me three minutes and we'll finish this divorce today. Let me talk to Carmen and the two attorneys in the next room — the library — and we'll be done."

The judge leaned back.

"Is that so, Mr. Kircaali?"

"Yes."

The four of us walked into the library.

I said the entire process was ridiculous and costing money by the minute.

"Here's what we're going to do. Carmen and I will split everything fifty-fifty. Cash, cars, all assets. I'll move to our Florida home. Carmen keeps the New Jersey house."

Then I added:

"Carmen, I'm going to step outside with my lawyer. You and your lawyer stay here and decide."

Her lawyer didn't hesitate.

"You don't need to wait. We agree."

We were back in the courtroom in under sixty seconds.

The judge looked at me with a condescending grin.

"So, Mr. Kircaali, did you finalize your divorce?"

Carmen's lawyer answered:

"Yes, Your Honor."

The judge signed the decree, stamped it with the golden seal, and that was it.

Now here's the part I didn't know at the time.

* * *

One day at the office, a woman pulled me aside.

"Fuat, I need to talk to you. Your divorce lawyer is my uncle — my mother's brother. And your judge is the girlfriend of his son."

Then she added:

"They were all together at our house for Christmas. My cousin broke up with her during Christmas dinner. She's very upset."

With that information — and perhaps influenced by too many courtroom scenes on television — after the judge handed our divorce papers to the attorneys, I said:

"Your Honor, may I approach the bench?"

She looked annoyed.

"What, Mr. Kircaali?"

In a voice loud enough for the entire courtroom to hear, I said:

"Now that we're divorced, may I take you out to dinner?"

I was escorted out of the courtroom.

Then out of the courthouse.

By two security officers.

* * *

The next morning, the women in the office were buzzing about Carmen's massive divorce party.

I turned to Carmen and said:

"Why wasn't I invited?"

She looked at me.

"I picked you up for every hearing and drove you back. I hear there was a private chef, a party tent attached to the living room, an open bar, and waiters in white gloves passing drinks and *hors d'oeuvres* to hundreds of guests — and I didn't even get an invite."

CHAPTER 36
I'm writing this book in
Nixon's library
where he wrote his memoirs.

Writing This Book in Nixon's Library

Our offices were almost all located along Chestnut Ridge Road — except for my home in Jersey City and our office at 39 East Central Avenue in Pearl River, New York, the building I bought from a pizza man after I got evicted from my townhouse for running an industrial-scale business out of my living room.

Our very first garage office was at 884 Chestnut Ridge Road in Chestnut Ridge, New York. From there, we moved to 135 Chestnut Ridge Road in Montvale, New Jersey. After our ten-year lease expired, we relocated once again — this time to 577 Chestnut Ridge Road in Woodcliff Lake, New Jersey.

For more than twenty years, we worked on the same road.

***

Just a few miles away, history had unfolded long before we arrived.

After the presidency, Richard Nixon spent a significant part of his post–White House life in Saddle River, New Jersey, where he retreated from public view and devoted himself to writing. Tucked into the quiet, wooded privacy of Bergen County, Nixon used the isolation of his estate to reflect, analyze, and attempt to rebuild his legacy through words.

During that time, he also rented an office at the Perillo Tours Plaza building.

There, he worked long hours dictating and revising manuscripts, transforming himself from a disgraced former president into one of the most prolific post-presidential authors in American history.

The calm of Saddle River offered something the White House never could:

silence — and the time to write.

***

I was also living in Saddle River at the time. Just down the street was Rocco Commisso, the richest man in New Jersey, and around the corner lived the Inserra family, owners of the ShopRite supermarket chain. One night, when Lawrence R. Inserra Sr. needed an ambulance, the town's only unit was out of service. After that experience, he donated two ambulances to the town.

That was my neighborhood.

***

Years later, when we moved into the Perillo Tours building ourselves, I asked Steve Perillo about the Nixon photos and memorabilia displayed in the lobby alongside his father, Mario Perillo.

Steve smiled and said, "Nixon's office was in this building. As a matter of fact, your office now was Nixon's library — where he wrote his memoirs."

Nixon's *Beyond Peace* (1994), his final book, offering policy ideas just weeks before his death, was written in that very library — my new office.

***

Nixon was also known to love Chinese food. After Jiang Zemin, the President of the People's Republic of China, paid a private visit to Nixon in Saddle River, a Chinese restaurant mysteriously opened in the small shopping plaza next to our office — the same space that had once housed Nixon's library.

The food was excellent.

An autographed photo of Nixon hung behind the cash register.

That spot is now a Fresh Market.

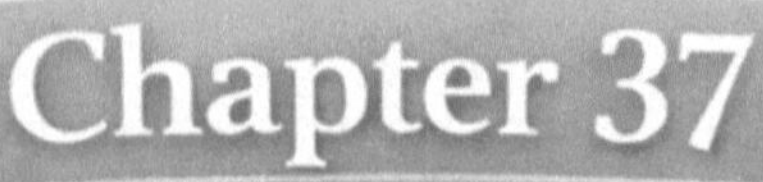

Chapter 37

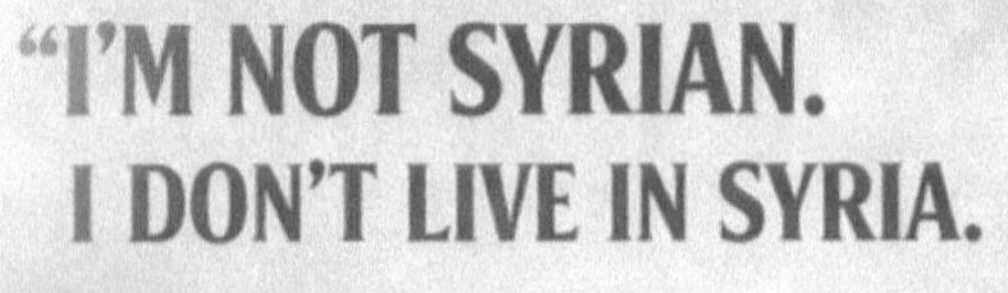

"I'M NOT SYRIAN.
I DON'T LIVE IN SYRIA.

SO HOW THE HELL
DID I END UP IGNITING

AN UPRISING AGAINST
Bashar al-Assad?"

Wikileaks

I'm not Syrian. I don't live in Syria.

So how the hell did I end up igniting an uprising against Bashar al-Assad?

Remember my "Ten Years, Five Wives" chapter?

At one point, I gathered my six-month-old daughter, her mother, and her grandmother, and we all moved into my deep-water house in Lighthouse Point, Florida—an address that, remarkably, still appears on my driver's license today.

From then on, I commuted to work from Florida.

Every Friday, I boarded a JetBlue flight south, anxious to see my baby.

Early Monday morning, I'd be back on the first flight out, heading to Montvale, New Jersey, to start the week all over again.

***

One Friday afternoon, I arrived home and the house was empty.

I asked my caretaker, Don, where everyone was. He told me that earlier that day, Grandma had cooked a big homemade meal for the whole crew—the landscapers, the pool guys, everyone. That was the last time he'd seen my family.

In short, her mother decided she didn't like America. She took our daughter and her own mother, and the three of them flew back to Aleppo, Syria.

Just like that, they were gone.

If you search online for "Fuat Kircaali, Florida man, Sofia," you'll find plenty of news coverage about what happened next.

***

One day, I was working at my Nixon Library office in Woodcliff Lake, New Jersey, when our receptionist, Edna, walked in.

"Fuat, two FBI agents want to see you," she said.

I told her, "Send them in."

Two agents introduced themselves. The one in charge was Byron Daniel. They said they needed to meet with me about an international case where they thought I could help, but since I didn't have high-level clearance, they couldn't discuss any details. All I gathered was that spies from two different countries were operating in the United States, and those countries were becoming a serious threat to Silicon Valley companies.

Some of those tech companies were exhibiting at our conference at the Javits Center the following week. The agents were especially interested in our registration list—20,000 attendees long.

We walked downstairs, and Krisandra exported a fresh registration file with full contact information and addresses. We handed it to Byron.

He also requested five attendee badges for the agents to attend the show. We issued full conference badges for all five.

***

My meetings with Byron lasted more than a year, until one day we were watching breaking news on *60 Minutes*. The FBI had just cracked a huge international spy case.

By then, we had become friends. I explained to him that I was about to travel to Syria. My daughter had been taken there by her mother, and the Syrian government had no intention of sending her back home.

Only a handful of countries in the world didn't recognize the Hague Convention on children abducted by a parent—places like Iran, North Korea, and Syria. That meant there was no legal treaty forcing them to return my daughter.

I explained to Byron that I had retained a former FBI agent—a specialist experienced in international kidnapping cases. We had used him earlier to uncover financial crimes as part of our news stories. A former high-level FBI executive, Mr. Black, I can't recall his first name, from the Miami area, was also approaching the situation from his own angle to help me.

I told Byron the only option I had at the moment was to create a Twitter account, @SyrianPresident, travel to Syria, and use the #Feb11 hashtag to encourage an uprising against the government.

At the time, he was a special agent on the Joint Terrorism Task Force in the Southern District of Manhattan.

***

While I was boarding my flight to Damascus at JFK, he called me and told me to make sure I deleted all my communication with the FBI—emails, text messages, contact records, business cards, everything. I did. He also said that if I needed help for any reason, I should go to the nearest U.S. embassy or consulate and ask for the FBI agent in charge, and not talk to anyone else.

At that moment, I realized I was being protected.

I made half a dozen welfare visits to Syria. On each trip, Syrian intelligence followed me from the moment I landed until the moment I left the country. Once, while I was out of my hotel room, they opened my camera, put in fresh batteries to check what was inside, and lost one of the dead ones. When I returned, I found that battery tucked inside my shoe.

****

My very own Twitter-fueled Syrian revolution started to gain traction. Protests across the cities accelerated. At some point, my daughter's mother had no choice but to leave the country. They took the last civilian flight from Aleppo to Cairo—the final flight out before everything shut down.

I flew to Cairo the next day and put them in a suite at the Sofitel Cairo Nile El Gezirah for six months. Then I brought them to Istanbul until I could arrange their visas back home.

****

Sometime later, the Wikileaks Syria Files emerged. My name was in them. The Syrian government had been making serious efforts to deal with me and my extracurricular activities in their country.

After the Wikileaks release, *The Guardian* ran a story about how Asma al-Assad, Bashar's wife, had personally worked for six months to persuade Twitter to suspend my @SyrianPresident parody account. She succeeded. I was no longer leading an uprising against her husband—but my mission had already been accomplished. I got my daughter out.

****

One day, I was driving to Key West when Byron called. I heard the news about Bin Laden from him before President Obama went on TV.

I owned my company again—100%—an
delivered our two best events with zero staf

When the Cook Quit

Carmen had a boyfriend who was, in polite terms, a knucklehead.

Let's call him Dr. Salvatore.

He wasn't very bright, but he was deeply impressed — especially by Carmen's lifestyle. When they met, he couldn't quite process how successful she was or where the money came from. Instead of asking questions, he jumped straight to a conclusion: if he married Carmen, he could become rich too.

In his mind, the formula was simple.

There had already been a Fuat and a Carmen. That partnership had built a real business. So why not recreate it?

His business model was essentially Fuat & Carmen 2.0 — except this time, he would be Fuat, and Carmen would be his business partner.

It sounded perfect.

The only problem was that neither of them had the slightest idea what the business would actually be — beyond becoming really, really rich.

After some brainstorming, they landed on what I came to call the neck business.

They preferred a more sophisticated name: relationship management.

There was no product.

No service.

Just talk, motivation, and promises.

Dr. Salvatore imagined himself as a motivational speaker — Tony Robbins, but better. At least in his own mind.

To get started, they needed capital.

That part wasn't difficult — at least not from his perspective. Carmen had millions in the bank. Once the business took off, he assured her, they would make millions more.

So she began investing her money into his ideas.

* * *

Dr. Salvatore — a foot doctor from a Caribbean medical school with a suspended medical license — suddenly became an entrepreneur at the age of sixty. One week he was pitching solar panels over the phone. The next week, he was hosting a podcast — in my New Jersey mansion — complete with drone shots flying into my living room as he opened his live show.

It was a major production.

With a major budget.

None of it made sense.

* * *

Dr. Salvatore would lean over to Carmen and say,

"Honey, when was the last time Fuat was at the office?"

She would answer,

"Maybe a year ago?"

He'd shake his head.

"Honey, you're working so hard. You're doing your job and his job, and he's keeping half the money. That's not fair to you."

Then he'd smile and seal it.

"Trust me. In our new business, it will just be you and me. No Fuat."

* * *

With this new man in her life, Carmen became confused. She wanted to believe in him — and in his so-called business ambitions. The distraction began to affect her focus at work.

At the time, I had a full staff on payroll producing two major events each year: New York at the Javits Center and Silicon Valley at the Santa Clara Convention Center, six months apart. These shows had to be sold, produced, and delivered with precision.

I may not have been physically in the office every day, but I was fully on top of the business. I worked online with every department, every manager, every decision.

Carmen was there in person with the team.

I was there everywhere else.

How would Dr. Salvatore know that?

He hadn't even figured out what I did for a living.

* * *

I was in Africa when I received Carmen's email.

Her husband, she wrote, needed a second hip surgery — both hips —

followed by a long and delicate recovery. She said she would need three months off.

Something didn't feel right.

I called Joan.

"There's no hip surgery," she said. "Sal is fine. He's at the gym every day lifting weights."

That's when the alarm bells went off.

* * *

I started digging.

What I discovered stunned me.

Dr. Salvatore and Carmen had quietly recruited my entire staff — people still on my payroll. The management photos and bios on their new website were my own employees.

Except I was still paying their salaries.

The photos were professionally produced. Dr. Salvatore sat on a couch in my New Jersey mansion like royalty, surrounded by my staff standing behind him.

Each of them had new titles.

New job descriptions.

All working for Dr. Salvatore's "neck business."

* * *

When I checked their social media accounts, I realized something even worse.

This hadn't just started.

It had been going on for years.

Around that same time, Carmen's daughter took over accounting from Joan after more than two decades. The money was now fully in the hands of Dr. Salvatore, Carmen, and her daughter.

That, too, had been happening for years.

This is what happens when you fully trust your partner.

* * *

I returned to Florida and soon received a call from the IRS.

At the Fort Lauderdale office, an agent opened my tax return, flipped to a page, and said,

"Do you see this section here — Schedule C rolling into Schedule D?"

I told her I didn't follow.

"That's fine," she said. "Put a yellow Post-it note on this page and take it to court. Tell the judge your partner has been taking hundreds of thousands of dollars from your business without your knowledge."

She paused.

"The judge will know exactly why I highlighted it."

The next day, Dr. Salvatore showed up unannounced in Florida.

He wanted to return the money.

No lawsuits.

No court.

I called my attorney, Alan Asher.

Within days, the paperwork was completed. Carmen's forty-nine percent ownership interest was returned to me.

Once again, I owned my company one hundred percent — just like day one.

* * *

That Friday, I emailed everyone in the office and fired them all.

Later that night, my parking-lot security camera recorded Dr. Salvatore walking out of the building at two in the morning — carrying the accounting computer.

I shut everything down.

* * *

I emptied the office.

Returned the keys to my landlord, Steve Perillo.

Paid the remaining rent balance.

I did it all remotely — from Florida.

Then I returned to Turkey to be with my daughter.

The timing couldn't have been better.

We were between our East Coast and West Coast events.

I arrived at my Istanbul apartment overlooking the Marmara Sea, opened my laptop, and sat quietly for a moment — taking in the view, the silence, and the reality that I was starting over again, just like in the old days.

With zero staff — a serious payroll savings, by the way — I secured my upcoming event dates. I had six months to deliver New York, and another six months after that to produce Silicon Valley.

On a six-month deadline, I delivered one of the best conferences of my career — entirely by myself — from that Istanbul apartment.

Conference program.

Ten simultaneous tracks.

Six keynotes.

Two hundred world-class speakers.

Faculty coordination.

Sponsorship and expo sales.

Freeman Decorating.

Delegate sales — $1,250 Gold Pass tickets.

Every detail an international conference requires — handled alone.

And it raised a question I asked myself every day:

Why did I ever need an entire staff?

Instead of explaining what people should be doing at their desks, I was simply doing the work myself — faster, better, and more efficiently.

With my ADHD and a slight touch of autism, the conference website looked better than it had in more than a decade.

Every email inquiry was answered within sixty seconds — one of the original rules I had set when I first launched the company.

For the first time in a long time, I was genuinely thrilled. It was a one-man show — and it worked beautifully.

During those months, Carmen kept asking people around me the same question:

"Who's producing this show?"

The answer never changed.

"Fuat is doing it himself. Every single detail. He has no staff."

She refused to believe it.

So she asked again.

"Who is running the show?"

Still, the answer stayed the same.

* * *

We delivered New York in November.

Next came Silicon Valley in June.

Throughout my career, I had always valued input from my team. Collaboration had built much of what we achieved.

But this time was different.

This show would be produced my way — no input needed.

* * *

I secured Expo Halls C and D — 43,652 square feet — and took ownership of the divider between them, creating one massive, uninterrupted footprint.

Hall C became the keynote hall, set banquet-style for 2,000 delegates.

Hall D — 21,828 square feet — became the expo floor.

It was bold.

It was expensive.

And it was exactly how I envisioned it.

* * *

I also secured fifteen meeting rooms for our twelve conference tracks.

The Silicon Valley event became the strongest show we had delivered at the Santa Clara Convention Center in more than two decades.

The expo floor sold out.

That afternoon, our blockchain keynote was livestreamed worldwide to more than 30,000 viewers, as Oracle used our stage to unveil its long-anticipated blockchain product.

Everything aligned — vision, execution, and timing.

* * *

My daughter, Sofia, worked the registration desk alongside a dozen agents. It ran more smoothly than any registration operation we had ever had at that venue.

Including the Freeman crew, audiovisual teams, and catering staff, more than one hundred people worked across the three days of the conference.

And somehow — from an apartment overlooking the Marmara Sea — I had produced and coordinated it all with zero full-time staff and no partner to share the profits with.

What ever happened to Dr. Salvatore and his neck business?

After years of halfhearted attempts, I believe he finally gave up — without generating a single cent of revenue. He's now back to selling solar panels to homeowners, which, ironically, is exactly what he was doing when the two of them first met — in his basement bedroom rental, wedged beside a garage.

* * *

As we packed up and headed to the airport in Santa Clara, Covid hit.

The world shut down for the next four years.

Lesson learned?

Maybe for everyone around me.

Never underestimate the owner who built the business from nothing.

The world may shut down.

Businesses may disappear.

But the man who built it once can always build it again.

ACT IV — REINVENTION

When everything stops, you learn what was real.

The world shut down. The calendar went blank. The engine that had carried me forward for decades suddenly went silent.

But motion doesn't disappear — it waits.

Stripped of titles, travel, stages, and schedules, I returned to something older than business. Older than success. Something rooted not in scale, but in instinct.

This final act isn't about rebuilding an empire.

It's about understanding why I kept building in the first place.

CHAPTER 39

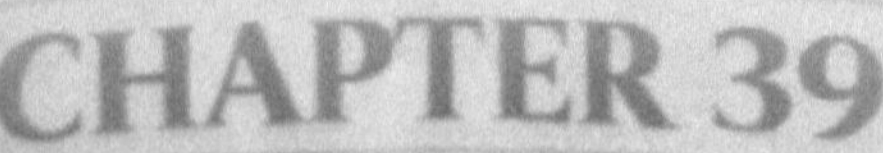

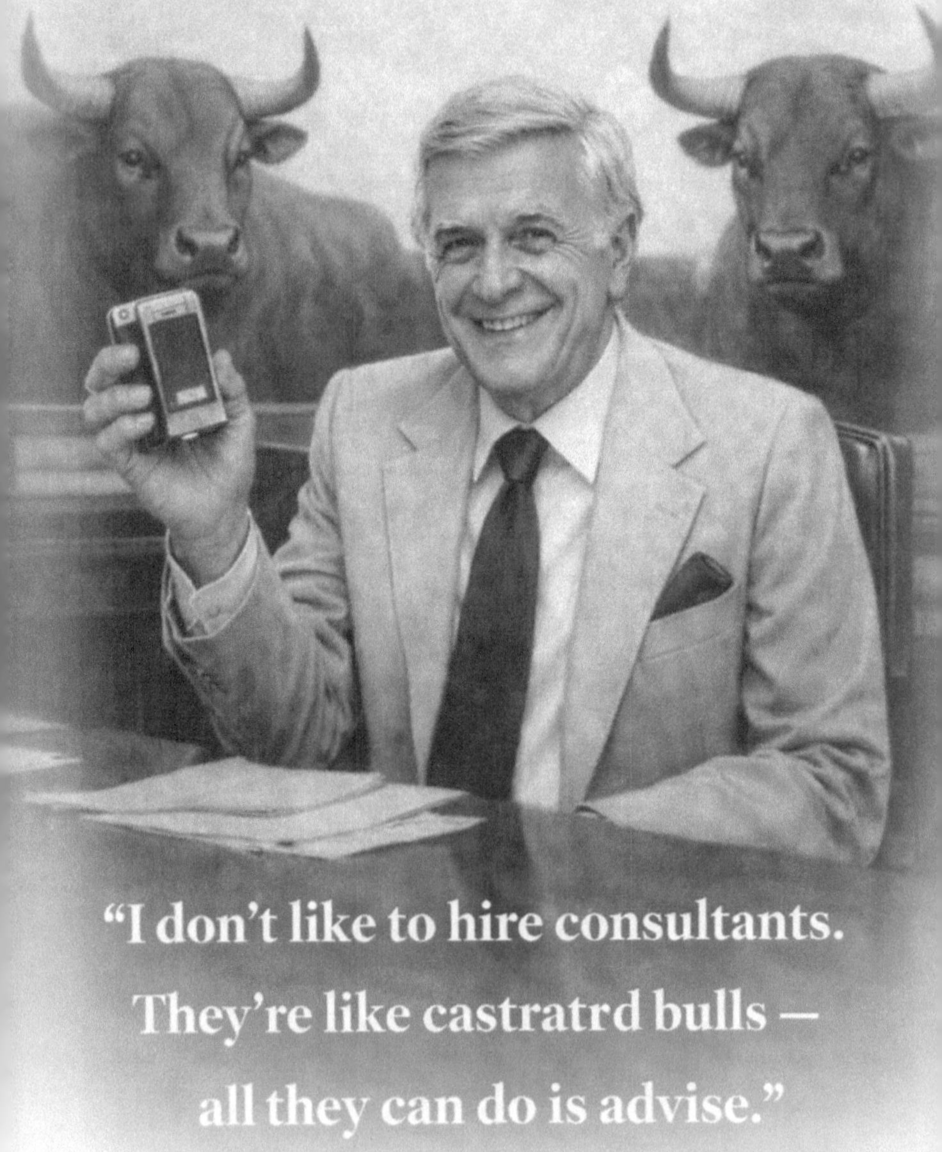

"I don't like to hire consultants. They're like castratrd bulls — all they can do is advise."

Castrated Bulls

When I arrived in the United States in 1984 and finally began finding my footing, three television commercials left a deep impression on me.

The first was Colonel Sanders doing his own KFC ads. I must have eaten more two-piece Original Recipe meals than I care to admit. The second was Mario Perillo — "Mr. Italy" — selling dream vacations with effortless confidence and charm.

Mario Perillo lived in Saddle River, New Jersey, the same town where I would later spend decades of my life.

He was a local celebrity. Everyone knew him from television.

The last time I saw him was at The Park Steakhouse in Park Ridge. He was dining quietly with his family. I stopped to pay my respects. He looked fragile.

Not long after that, we heard the news of his passing.

* * *

Years later, in one of life's small coincidences, I became a tenant of his son, Steve Perillo, at the Perillo Tours Plaza building — where I remained for nearly ten years.

SYS-CON Media and Cloud Expo, Inc. were headquartered at 577 Chestnut Ridge Road in Woodcliff Lake, New Jersey. But the commercial that stayed with me most was different. It was the man who liked a shaving machine so much, he bought the company. That man was Victor Kiam.

* * *

While browsing the business section at Barnes & Noble, I picked up two of his books and read them with genuine pleasure. He spoke plainly, without pretense, and his confidence felt earned. One line especially stayed with me:

"I don't like to hire consultants. They're like castrated bulls — all they can do is advise."

* * *

Victor Kiam was one of those larger-than-life business figures everyone seemed to know in the 1980s. His famous line — "I liked it so much, I bought the company" — wasn't marketing fluff. It was exactly how he lived.

After trying a Remington electric razor, he purchased the struggling company in 1979 and turned it around completely.

What made the story unforgettable was that he didn't hide behind agencies or actors — he became the spokesman himself. He looked straight into the camera and sold the product like a real businessman, not a performer.

It worked.

Remington went from losing money to becoming a global brand.

* * *

Kiam became a celebrity not because he chased fame, but because he believed in what he was selling. He even delivered commercials in multiple languages overseas. For a time, he was everywhere.

Later, he bought the New England Patriots — a move that didn't end well — but that never changed how I saw him. To me, Victor Kiam represented something rare: conviction.

When he believed in something, he went all in — publicly, personally, and without apology.

He wasn't perfect.

But he was real.

And in business, that kind of authenticity is harder to find than talent.

* * *

Two of his memoirs I read more than once. His books became a subliminal guide during my own business journey.

Harvard Business School cannot make you a *bakkal*.

A Bakkal During COVID

The federal Public Health Emergency remained in effect from January 2020 until May 11, 2023 — a period of roughly three years and four months.

So did anyone really expect me to sit at home doing nothing for three years?

Never.

My show business was finished overnight. No hotels. No airline travel. No conferences. No expos. Everything that powered my life — and my income — simply stopped.

And the truth is, I didn't need to work. I already had my life savings.

But then ask yourself this: why is Warren Buffett still working at ninety-five? He doesn't need to either.

Fine.

But I was a bakkal in my DNA.

Bakkal is a Turkish word for a neighborhood convenience-store owner — the guy who opens early, closes late, and always finds a way to make something work. You're either born a bakkal or you're not. You can't study it. You can't learn it. It's instinct.

Harvard Business School cannot make you a bakkal.

The English word is entrepreneur, but I hate that term. It comes with a sense of entitlement, as if success is somehow owed to you.

I don't use it.

* * *

So I found things to do during those three years.

The first business was urgent.

Purell ran out of product. Hand sanitizer disappeared everywhere. Overnight, the country had a shortage.

I put together a production assembly line — fast — and started manufacturing hand sanitizer in ten-ounce clear bottles. I'm sure many people had the same idea, but execution wasn't easy. Finding containers was nearly impossible.

I tracked down a supplier in mainland China, literally filled an entire UPS plane with bottles, and flew them into Florida.

Then I located alcohol in Tennessee.

The first tanker arrived at my facility carrying 6,000 gallons of hand-sanitizer-grade alcohol. We emptied it into nineteen 330-gallon IBC totes — giant square industrial containers stacked like silent witnesses to what desperation can create. During our first alcohol delivery, a neighbor called the Pompano Beach Fire Department. Until ATF agents sorted out what we were actually doing inside the warehouse, my crew was arrested and taken into custody. I went and bailed them out.

* * *

I'll skip most of the timeline here.

In short, our Purell-efficacy hand sanitizer — fully lab-tested and certified — became a bestseller on Amazon.

While Amazon shipments ran on autopilot, I hired much of the unemployed kitchen staff and servers from the Red Fox Diner next door.

* * *

Then I decided to do something completely different.

I bought a teardown waterfront property and designed and built what I believed would be one of the most beautiful homes in the world.

TikTok and YouTube channels agreed. They literally called it "one of the most beautiful homes in the world." They wanted it to go viral — and it did. Millions watched my marketing videos.

I listed the property for $7.9 million and sold it for cash to a twenty-five-year-old Bitcoin kid.

* * *

Toward the end of the COVID years, I launched a soft-wash business franchise. Florida, Georgia, New York, New Jersey, Connecticut, and Los Angeles became our service areas during the first year.

That business is still operating today, with one simple goal:

to clean every roof in America.

* * *

Conclusion

COVID shut the world down.

It didn't shut me down.

When everything stopped,

I didn't wait.

I didn't panic.

I didn't complain.

I built.

Because some people need stability to move forward.

Others need chaos.

And a bakkal doesn't wait for normal to return.

He opens the store —

even when the lights are out,

the street is empty,

and everyone else is still at home.

CHAPTER 42

“Plop, plop, *fizz, fizz,* *oh what a relief it is*”

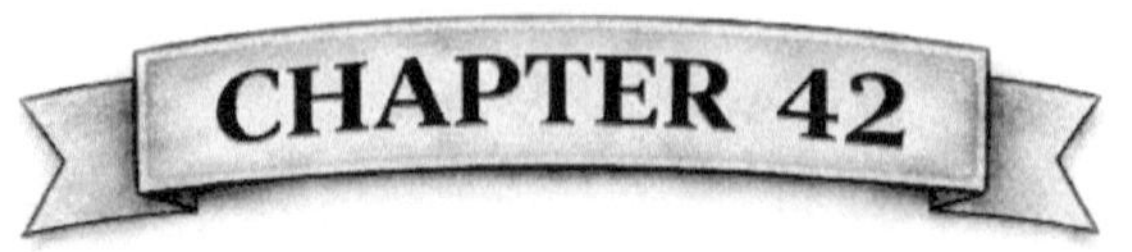

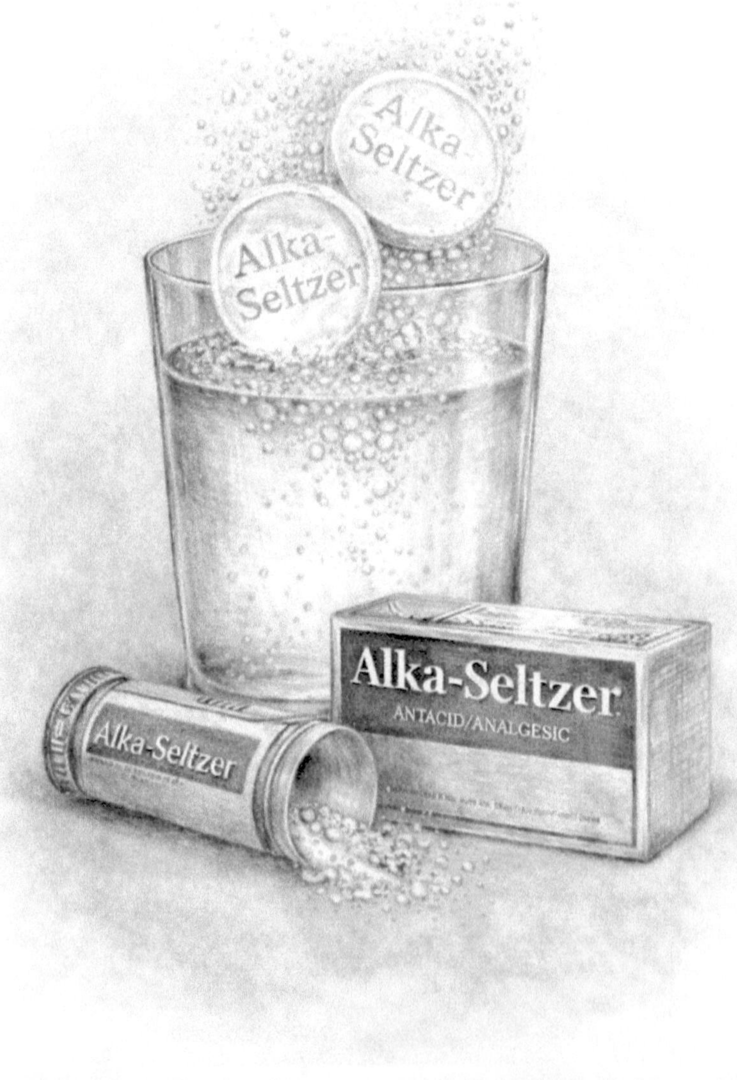

The Truth Behind My Dumb Luck

 ere's the spoiler alert after all the chapters that came before: my business journey—which ended up taking up most of my adult life—wasn't a lottery ticket.

I was ready for it.

Big time.

This wasn't a get-rich-quick story.

When I announced my first magazine, I wasn't dreaming about a new game console or a sports car. In my professional software-developer world, I was admiring *Paradox User's Journal*. That was my inspiration. Not something flashy or glamorous—just a solid, boring, professional publication that people actually needed.

Carmen would always warn people, "Don't let him fool you—he's sharper than he looks."

I don't know about sharp. I was sharp, yes—but more importantly, I was obsessively passionate, fueled by what I now recognize as self-diagnosed ADHD and a touch of autism. Once I locked onto something, there was no letting go.

Why was I so fixated on dreaming about a magazine?

It goes back to my childhood.

I won't bore you with all the details, but here's the short version of what quietly set me up for all of this.

When I was six or seven years old, I would take a single sheet of copy paper, fold it into quarters—eight tiny pages—and stitch it along the spine like a real newsletter. Then I'd create a miniature magazine with a pencil and hand it to family members, one at a time, waiting patiently while they read every single page.

Back then there were no reams of paper sitting around. If a store ordered supplies, it might receive a bundle of five hundred sheets—but you didn't buy them that way. You bought one sheet for five cents and carried it home carefully, doing your best not to wrinkle it.

Over time I got more ambitious. I started laying out columns, mimicking the look of real newsletters and magazines.

I even added ad pages.

By middle school, I had invented my first printing press.

I nailed four pieces of wood into a frame the size of a sheet of paper and stretched silk cloth across it. I typed my columns onto carbon paper, turning the letters into tiny holes—very similar to how T-shirt silk printing works today. When I poured black ink onto the silk frame, with my carbon template underneath, the page appeared in print.

There were no copy machines back then.

I'm talking about fifty or sixty years ago, in a small mountain village in Turkey.

That's when my classmate, Nezih Erdoğan, saw my makeshift newsletters. He had an instinctive understanding of fonts. He began hand-lettering my headlines in different styles—bold, italic, large, small—whatever the page needed.

Suddenly my silk-printed front-and-back newsletters were starting to look real.

And very cool.

***

Around the same time, I started fiddling with drawing cartoons. I submitted a few to national humor magazines, and one of them—with massive circulation—actually printed my cartoon on the back cover.

That magazine was *GırGır*.

Every Friday the entire country waited for it to hit the newsstands. I'm not exaggerating—the entire country.

Years later I asked ChatGPT to describe *GırGır*, and it summed it up perfectly: it was one of the most influential humor and satire magazines in Turkey—and, at its peak, one of the highest-circulation satire magazines in the world.

The magazine paid me 75 Turkish liras for the cartoon they published in 1972—about ₺1,144 in today's money.

I was thirteen years old.

My daily school allowance at the time? Twenty-five cents.

Soon three major humor magazines were regularly publishing my cartoons. At school I became a minor celebrity. Kids would point and whisper, "That's the kid—the cartoonist."

I was lucky in another way, too. I wasn't the class valedictorian, but I had access to a solid education—from elementary school all the way to Boğaziçi University, and later, briefly, a doctoral program at the University of Zurich.

Sixty years later, I still remember the words of our elementary school principal. He used to tell us:

"Every night before you go to bed, ask yourself: What did I learn today? Never let a day pass without an answer."

I still haven't.

***

When I graduated from high school and moved to Istanbul for college, I found a new playground.

Babıali Yokuşu—the street where nearly all the newspapers and magazines were clustered—became my daily destination.

With persistence and a lot of walking up and down that hill, I eventually became a regular contributor to several publications.

By 1976, at just seventeen years old, I was officially on the payroll at *Cumhuriyet* as an editorial cartoonist. I reported to Doğan Hızlan. My work appeared alongside artists like Turhan Selçuk and Ali Ulvi.

Cumhuriyet was one of Turkey's most important and historic newspapers—a symbol of secular, republican journalism. Founded in 1924 by Yunus Nadi, a close ally of Atatürk, it was not a small place to land—especially at seventeen.

I officially spent four years in college—though in reality it stretched to five—and most of that time was lived on Babıali Yokuşu.

After classes and work, I found myself surrounded by the giants of Turkish media.

I carried a Leica camera case for Ara Güler on photo shoots for years, served tea to Yaşar Kemal at the newspaper, and quietly stepped aside when the paper's owner, Nadir Nadi—often accompanied by his wife, Berin Nadi—walked into his office.

Dinner invitations came just as casually—to the homes of İlhan Selçuk, Turhan Selçuk, Yıldız Kenter, Cemal Süreya, Ali Ulvi, often Selim İleri, and many others.

Most of the poets and novelists who would later become household names were, at the time, simply working at the paper as copy editors.

I even found myself sitting in Sabahattin Ali's house during a jury meeting to select the annual best novel.

That year's winner was Orhan Pamuk.

Around the dinner table, no one had ever heard his name.

Years later, he would win the Nobel Prize.

To me, it all felt normal.

Only much later did I realize what an extraordinary education it really was.

I attended Boğaziçi University and graduated with a degree in Business Administration. Boğaziçi offered one of the best business education programs in the world, and the university was consistently ranked among the top 200 globally.

My childhood experience as a talented shoe salesman in my father's store had already given me a practical education in sales, marketing, advertising, and production planning long before I arrived at the university.

At Boğaziçi, I took advanced marketing classes with the world-famous Professor Mustafa Dilber. We studied countless case studies, including Sears, Roebuck & Co. and its famous promise: "Satisfaction guaranteed or your money back." We also analyzed the AMC case study and examined classic advertising campaigns, including the Alka-Seltzer commercial whose iconic jingle became part of American culture:

"Plop, plop, fizz, fizz, oh what a relief it is."

I also learned production planning and the concept of the critical path in manufacturing, including the mathematical calculations behind it.

All of this while I was still a teenager in the Turkish mountains who had never even been to America—learning the critical details of how large corporations were built and turned into giants.

I also took literature classes from Oya Başak, who introduced us to Oscar Wilde, John Keats, and the sonnets of William Shakespeare. We had to memorize them by heart.

Let me not to the marriage of true minds

Admit impediments. Love is not love

Which alters when it alteration finds,

Or bends with the remover to remove.

O no! it is an ever-fixed mark...

And of course there was Samuel Taylor Coleridge's *The Rime of the Ancient Mariner* (1798):

"Water, water, everywhere,

Nor any drop to drink."

***

As a child, I rarely went out to the street to play soccer with the other kids.

Instead, my father filled my world with books and ideas.

When I started high school, he bought me an entire set of the *Encyclopaedia Britannica*. He also subscribed me to *Time* magazine.

After school, I would walk to his shop, where he sold children's shoes.

Every Tuesday my personal copy of that week's *Time* magazine was waiting for me. I read each issue cover to cover and carefully saved them all in mint condition.

My father also subscribed me to the *Unforgettable Composers* series. Once a month an LP would arrive—Mozart, Beethoven, Dvořák—eventually more than fifty composers.

That became my soundtrack.

My father had emigrated as a teenager with his parents and siblings from Kırcaali. Like many Bulgarian immigrants in Turkey, they didn't look for jobs—they built businesses.

Some small, some large, but always their own.

Whether it was in my genes or simply learned behind the counter, I became a skilled salesman in my father's shoe store by the time I was fifteen.

The rule was simple:

Be honest.

Sell the best shoes the customer could find anywhere.

At a fair price—the same price for everyone.

No traditional Turkish bargaining.

So—dumb luck?

No.

It wasn't dumb luck at all.

CHAPTER 42

High School Reunion

High School Reunion

I happened to be in my hometown during our 40th high school reunion.

It turned out to be unexpectedly therapeutic.

We danced to the music of our youth — *Hotel California*, *The Wall*, Supertramp — the disco years that once felt endless. Almost everyone was there.

At one point, I walked toward two of my childhood friends. We were born on the same street, just a few houses apart — boys who grew up sharing the same sidewalks, the same summers, the same dreams of getting out.

As I approached the ballroom windows where they were standing, I overheard their conversation.

"Vasıf," Atilla asked, "how many passengers does your plane carry?"

"Twelve," Vasıf replied. Then he smiled. "How many does yours?"

"Six," Atilla said.

Vasıf immediately flashed victory signs with both hands, as if he'd just won a high-stakes bet.

Atilla paused, then added quietly,
"But I have two of them."

We have a high school group chat.
We stay in touch as much as life allows.

Whenever someone travels to New York, I pick him up at the airport and take him to his hotel. We usually meet for dinner around their business schedules. On one of those JFK runs, Atilla arrived with two younger men in dark suits. I dropped all three of them at the Waldorf Astoria.

That entire week, I didn't hear a word from him. They were completely tied up in meetings. On Friday, I flew to Puerto Rico for the weekend.

When I arrived at my hotel, my phone rang. It was Atilla.

"Are you alive?" I asked.

He laughed. "I waited for the market to close. Now it's safe to tell you."

Then he said it calmly, almost casually.

"I bought Godiva Chocolates for one billion dollars. The press release goes out Monday."

I wished him a safe trip home.

Vasıf, with his twelve-passenger plane, went on to build much of Moscow City's high-rise skyline on a fifty-year land lease.

Levent — whose name I mentioned earlier on that deserted island in the Bahamas — packaged the company he took over as CEO and sold it five years later for $900 million.

Some of my childhood friends have far more interesting stories to tell.

They just didn't write the book.

CHAPTER 43

Post-Production Notes

I started writing this book in my office at the Perillo Tours building, 577 Chestnut Ridge Road, Woodcliff Lake, New Jersey — once home to Richard Nixon's former library. Ironically, he wrote his own memoirs in those same surroundings.

Apparently, history enjoys the most luxurious real estate in town.

I finished the book at a Turkish coffee shop in Paterson, New Jersey, during the blizzard of 2026. That coffee shop — and its entire crew — kept me warm with the best Turkish tea and clean ashtrays after every Virginia Super Slim burn.

I met wonderful people there: Kadir, Özcan, Hasan, Selim — the entire crew. At some point, I stopped being a customer and became part of the furniture.

Even while I'm typing these lines on my phone right now they have no idea what I'm busy with on my phone.

I shared one of the final manuscripts with Louis.

I told him his name kept popping up throughout the book. I said readers would be very curious about who Louis was, and I promised I would include his photo — "The Louis."

He said, "If you're ever in New York, we'll take new photos. I've got all new photo and video gear now. Armed to the teeth."

This was slightly reassuring and slightly concerning.

I'm still not sure whether the final cover photo will come from his new studio or whether I'll end up using one we already have.

Publishing, like life, is often decided at the very last minute.

I also wrote several chapters in the Wegmans parking lot while waiting to pick up Sofi.

I discovered a perfect spot facing the Chase branch — the morning sun rising behind it, creating just the right lighting inside the car. It was cinematic.

If anyone had walked by with a camera, I would've assumed Netflix was calling.

Wegmans also has some of the best coffee around — certainly better than Starbucks.

For about three months, I even became friends with the coffee staff. At one point, they stopped asking my name and just nodded. That's when you know you're there too often.

During the final stages of production, we moved from the Reedsy platform to Atticus while keeping the same overall look and feel of the book.

We tested a 6 × 9 trim size, but it felt too bulky for a pocket-style memoir — more "airport textbook" than "read this on a plane."

So we settled on this 5.5 × 8.5 format instead.

I also ordered three copies of Victor Kiam's memoir — two paperbacks and one hardcover — to study the layout, pacing, and overall structure.

This is what authors call "research," and what spouses usually call "more books."

The main reason for switching to Atticus was flexibility.

We ran into a limitation with Reedsy: chapters were meant to open on odd-numbered pages, with chapter illustrations printed on the facing left page.

Reedsy didn't allow that level of control.

Atticus did.

Score one for layout nerds.

One of the final steps in post-production was securing our ISBN numbers.

When we called Bowker — after nearly ten years — John Tabeling looked up our account and said, "You have 110 ISBNs. Let me check."

They were all books and CDs. I didn't realize they are here in New Jersey.

I paused for a moment and thought, *wow — I didn't realize we had been that busy with publishing too.*

Somehow, I had managed to forget an entire career while writing a memoir about my life.

After resetting a few long-forgotten passwords — which required more patience than writing several chapters — we assigned the ISBN for *Dumb Luck*.

It should be live and fully registered within a couple of weeks.

Dumb Luck is going out with four ISBNs, covering both Ingram and KDP distribution. KDP will use our official ISBN, cataloged worldwide

— important for libraries, bookstores, and anyone who still believes books should exist physically.

Each language edition will be available in paperback and hardcover. This making the book four different products.

You'll be able to order it on Amazon with next-day shipping, or find it in the Business / Self-Help section of Barnes & Noble.

I've already gotten into trouble more than once at Barnes & Noble — in Boca Raton and on Route 17 in Paramus, New Jersey — after reorganizing their periodicals section by moving all twelve of my magazine titles to the front row of Computers & Software.

Technically, I was "helping."

No promises that I won't do it again with my own book.

I will, however, arrange a proper book signing at Barnes & Noble Paramus.

After thirty years as one of their magazine publishers, I think I've earned that.

And yes — I fully intend to bring a mountain of hardcover copies and stack them right at the entrance.

Old habits die hard.

Epilogue

People still ask the same question.

How did it happen?

Two hundred million dollars.

Twenty years.

A media company that seemed to appear out of nowhere.

Some expect a complicated answer — a brilliant strategy, a secret formula, a carefully engineered plan.

The truth is far less impressive.

Most of the time, I had no idea what I was doing.

***

When I stepped off the plane at JFK in 1984, I didn't arrive with a business plan or a dream of building a media empire.

I arrived with a suitcase, a few phone numbers, and the vague belief that something good might happen if I kept moving.

So I moved.

I said yes to things before I fully understood them.

Yes to starting a magazine when I had never published one.

Yes to organizing conferences when I had never run an event.

Yes to opportunities that looked slightly insane at the time.

Sometimes those decisions worked.

Sometimes they didn't.

But they kept the story moving forward.

***

Years later, when the numbers were added up — the magazines, the conferences, the companies built and sold — people started calling it success.

Others called it luck.

Maybe they were both right.

But luck has a funny habit of showing up only after a very long stretch of persistence.

Luck doesn't answer the phone at two in the morning.

Luck doesn't stay awake laying out magazines on a kitchen table.

Luck doesn't keep going when common sense says you probably shouldn't.

Momentum does.

And once momentum starts, it becomes difficult to stop.

***

Looking back now, the story still feels almost impossible to believe.

The immigrant with no plan.

The first magazine printed with money he didn't have.

The company that somehow grew into a global business.

None of it was predictable.

None of it followed a script.

But maybe that's exactly what made it work.

***

Because the best stories rarely begin with certainty.

They begin with motion.

One step.

Then another.

Then another.

And somewhere along the way, what looked like chaos slowly turns into a life.

***

People call that luck.

I call it motion.

Acknowledgments

This book exists because many people crossed my path before I understood what any of it would become.

Some offered guidance.

Some offered opportunity.

Some offered resistance — which turned out to be just as important.

Carmen stands at the center of this story. Long before there was structure or certainty, she believed in forward motion. When ideas arrived faster than explanations, she trusted the direction even when the destination was unclear. Much of what follows would not exist without her steadiness.

To the colleagues who worked beside me — often under impossible deadlines and uncertain conditions — thank you for choosing commitment over comfort. You built more than products. You built momentum.

To the writers, editors, speakers, exhibitors, and readers who trusted a young company that was still inventing itself, your belief arrived before credibility did. That faith mattered more than you may have realized at the time.

To the competitors who doubted us, you sharpened us.

To the failures that arrived uninvited, you taught lessons success never could.

And to the road — the long drives that gave me quiet when the world was loud — thank you for the space to think.

This book is not a celebration of outcomes, but of movement.

If any part of it resonates, the credit belongs to everyone who helped keep it in motion.

About the author

Fuat Kircaali is an entrepreneur and publisher who founded SYS-CON Media, a global technology publishing company that produced magazines, conferences, and events for the software industry.

During the 1990s and early 2000s, SYS-CON Media organized major technology conferences and published magazines read by developers and technology professionals around the world.

DUMB LUCK: Inside SYS-CON Media tells the true story of that journey — from arriving in the United States as an immigrant with almost no money to building an international technology media company.

Today, Fuat Kircaali continues to work on new ventures and writes about entrepreneurship, technology, and business.

You can read more stories and articles at:

www.sys-con.com

Fuat Kircaali lives in the United States and continues to write and build new ventures.

ALSO BY THE AUTHOR

How to Build a Magazine Empire
with No Money, No Investors, and No Safety Net

www.sys-con.com

What if you could launch a magazine with no capital, no investors, and no safety net—and still build it into a thriving media empire?

In *The Zero-Dollar Publisher*, Fuat Kircaali reveals the real-world playbook behind one of the most unlikely success stories in modern publishing. Starting from scratch, with nothing but determination and a maxed-out credit card, he built a global technology media company that produced magazines, conferences, and industry-defining events around the world.

This is not a theory book. It's a street-level guide to how publishing actually works—how to pick a market, sell advertising before your first issue, control costs, build circulation, and grow a brand into a profitable business.

Packed with hard-earned lessons, blunt advice, and practical strategies, *The Zero-Dollar Publisher* is for anyone who wants to launch a magazine, build a media brand, or create a business from nothing.

No money.
No investors.
No safety net.
Just results.

ALSO BY THE AUTHOR

TRADE SHOW GOLD

How to Launch & Profit From
High-Revenue Events

Trade shows can be some of the most profitable businesses in the world—if you know how to build them.

In *Trade Show Gold*, media entrepreneur Fuat Kircaali shares the real-world strategies behind launching high-revenue conferences and exhibitions from the ground up. Starting with small pilot events and growing them into industry-defining shows, he reveals how trade shows are created, sold, scaled, and turned into major profit centers.

This is not theory. It's a practical, step-by-step look at how to pick the right topic, secure sponsors, sell booths, attract attendees, and control costs—often before the first event even opens its doors.

Packed with hard-earned lessons and insider tactics, *Trade Show Gold* is a straightforward guide for publishers, entrepreneurs, and anyone looking to build a profitable event business.

Big revenue.

Smart positioning.

Events that pay for themselves—and then some.

Index

D

E

S

T

U

V

W

Before You Go

If you enjoyed reading DUMB LUCK: Inside SYS-CON Media, I would truly appreciate a short review on Amazon.

Reviews help other readers discover the story, and even a few words make a difference.

You can leave a review here:

Amazon.com

Thank you for taking the time to read this story.

— Fuat Kircaali

www.ingramcontent.com/pod-product-compliance
Lightning Source LLC
Chambersburg PA
CBHW021230060726
47590CB00005B/1706